W. B.
SELECTI

William Butler Yeats, son ... born near Dublin in 1865. In ... became interested in occultism and theosophy, and began writing plays, ballads and poetry. He wrote many of his plays for the Abbey Theatre, Dublin, the Irish national theatre he had helped to found. Though never abandoning symbolism, Yeats's later poetry became increasingly hard-edged and realistic. His later work also included *A Vision* – his philosophical treatise – and three volumes of autobiography. W. B. Yeats was awarded the Nobel Prize in 1923 and died in 1939 in the south of France. His grave is near Sligo, Ireland.

Pg. 99.   44.
   100.   65.
   112.
   153.
   104.

W.B. Yeats
Selected Poetry

edited with an introduction and notes by
A. Norman Jeffares
formerly Professor of English Studies, University of Stirling

Pan Books in association with
Macmillan London

This selection first published 1962 by Macmillan London Ltd
This revised edition published 1990 by
Pan Books Ltd,
Cavaye Place, London SW10 9PG,
in association with Macmillan London Ltd
9 8
Selection and editorial matter
© A. Norman Jeffares and Macmillan & Co Ltd 1962, 1990
ISBN 0 330 31520 X
Printed and bound in Great Britain by
Cox & Wyman Ltd, Reading, Berkshire

CONTENTS

From IN THE SEVEN WOODS (1904) —

From THE GREEN HELMET AND OTHER POEMS
    (1910) —

CONTENTS

From A FULL MOON IN MARCH (1935) —

From LAST POEMS (1936–1939) —

INTRODUCTION

William Butler Yeats (1865–1939) was the eldest son of John Butler Yeats, whose family came to Ireland from Yorkshire in the seventeenth century. Jervis Yeats, the earliest known of the family, was a linen merchant in Dublin, as were his son Benjamin and his grandson, also christened Benjamin. The family gave up trade on the failure of the grandson's business. His son became Rector of Drumcliff, in Co. Sligo, and his grandson, William Butler Yeats, Rector of Tullylish, Co. Down. John Butler Yeats, William Butler's son, was also destined for the church, but he found he had no religious belief and became a barrister. In 1862 he went on a visit to Sligo in the north-west of Ireland to visit an old schoolfriend, George Pollexfen, fell in love with one of his sisters, Susan Mary, and married her in 1863. Later he was to say of his eldest son that by marriage to a Pollexfen he had given a tongue to the sea cliffs. The Yeatses and the Pollexfens were certainly very different: the Yeatses talkative, kind, imaginatively creative, and careless about money; the Pollexfens silent, dour, factually materialistic. The latter owned mills and a shipping company in Sligo and at first they welcomed the young John Butler Yeats, a landlord (with 300 acres of land in Kildare that had come into the family by the last of the linen drapers marrying a well-to-do Butler of the great Anglo-Irish Ormonde family), who was reading for the Bar.

When their son-in-law rejected a career in law in favour of becoming an artist, the Pollexfens began to wonder what their daughter had done, and to criticize him openly when John Butler Yeats did not show signs of becoming a financially successful artist. As money became scarce (the Kildare lands were heavily mortgaged) the artist's wife and children stayed in Sligo with her parents for extended periods. For the children

Sligo seemed home. William Butler was followed by Susan Mary (Lily), Elizabeth Corbet (Lottie), Robert Corbet (Bobbie) who died at the age of three, John Butler (Jack) who was to become a famous Irish painter, and Grace, who died before she was a year old.

The artist established various households in London – at Edith Villas, North End, west Kensington, from Autumn 1874 to Spring 1879, then at Woodstock Road, Bedford Park, until Autumn 1881, when he moved the family to Balscaddan Cottage at Howth. The family next moved to Island View, overlooking Howth Harbour, in 1882, and then to Ashfield Road in Harold's Cross, a Dublin suburb, in 1884. In London Willie went to the Godolphin School at Hammersmith from January 1877 to Easter 1881, in Dublin to the Erasmus Smith High School from Autumn 1881 to December 1883. He was described as a white blackbird among the others at the latter school, following his own bent and surprising his schoolfellows by his reading in Huxley and Haeckel, in Darwin and Wallace.

His enthusiasm for science was not long lasting. He had begun to write poetry in his late teens, enthusiastically encouraged by his father, who had declaimed poetry aloud to his son (always selecting its most passionate moment) when they took the train from Howth into Dublin, the one to his studio, the other to his school. The artist's scepticism soon surfaced in his son; paradoxically, while wanting to have a faith, to be able to believe, he could not lay aside his questioning, his need for proof, for evidence. After leaving the High School Willie entered the School of Art in Dublin. (Some doubt existed about whether he could pass the entrance examination to Trinity College, where his father, grandfather and great-grandfather had been students, though shortage of money may also have been a reason, as well as his father's dislike of the academic atmosphere in Trinity.) There he met George Russell, later to be known as AE, with whom he shared an interest in mysticism and the supernatural.

In Sligo, where fairy and folk tales dealt with the mysterious otherworld, with ghosts and apparitions, belief in the supernatural was common. The contrast between the practical doings of the Pollexfens and the Yeatses' endless discussion of ideas was reinforced by other equally powerful contrarieties: not only life in the city as opposed to the country, but the differing attitudes Yeats had found in London and Sligo. His English schoolfellows, in their desire to get on in life, had seemed merely materialistic; his father, however, thought a gentleman should not be concerned with getting on. Yet his own inability to order his life, to provide money for his family, strengthened his son's desire to make something of his life. At his English school he had thought that if when he grew up he was as clever among grown-up men as he was among these boys he would be a famous man.

His early poetry was romantic, Spenser and Shelley and the pre-Raphaelites his models. Spanish or Indian settings, however, gave way to Irish when he began to find in Ireland lasting subject matter and to develop his own individual style. He had an Irish audience in mind when, like William Allingham, he wrote about places in the west of Ireland, when he drew upon the fairy and folk tales he had heard in Sligo, and when he began to read translations of Irish literature, particularly of the epic tales of the Ulster saga and the tales of the Fianna. He was introduced to this literature by John O'Leary, an old Fenian leader who returned to Dublin in 1885, after serving some years of a prison sentence which had been commuted to exile. O'Leary's influence replaced that of his father, and Yeats became increasingly interested in nationalist politics. He formed the idea of recreating a specifically Irish literature which would give dignity to Ireland's idea of itself, by making Irish readers aware of their heritage of a Gaelic civilization, by encouraging a new literature not dominated by political rhetoric but distinctively heroic in its return to past traditions.

His own imagination caught fire. In *The Wanderings of Oisin* he showed the emotive and strange force of the Irish legends. This long poem of three parts tells how Oisin, the son of the hero Finn, the leader of the Fianna, spends three hundred years with the immortal Niamh in the Isles of the Living, of Victories and Forgetfulness. On his return to Ireland, having found none of his old companions, he is about to return to Niamh, his fairy bride. But his years suddenly descend upon him when he forgets Niamh's instruction not to touch the ground, and he confronts the Christianity of St Patrick defiantly. The poem is rich in decoration, its has a languorous beauty, but it also tells its story effectively; and it shows how original and accomplished a poet Yeats had become at twenty-three. Here is a passage from Book I of *The Wanderings of Oisin* (ll. 132–64).

Oisin. We galloped over the glossy sea:
   I know not if days passed or hours,
   And Niamh sang continually
   Danaan songs, and their dewy showers
   Of pensive laughter, unhuman sound,
   Lulled weariness, and softly round
   My human sorrow her white arms wound.
   We galloped; now a hornless deer
   Passed by us, chased by a phantom hound
   All pearly white, save one red ear;
   And now a lady rode like the wind
   With an apple of gold in her tossing hand;
   And a beautiful young man followed behind
   With quenchless gaze and fluttering hair.

'Were these two born in the Danaan land,
   Or have they breathed the mortal air?'

'Vex them no longer,' Niamh said,
   And sighing bowed her gentle head,
   And sighing laid the pearly tip
   Of one long finger on my lip.

But now the moon like a white rose shone
In the pale west, and the sun's rim sank,
And clouds arrayed their rank on rank
About his fading crimson ball:
The floor of Almhuin's hosting hall
Was not more level than the sea,
As, full of loving fantasy,
And with low murmurs, we rode on,
Where many a trumpet-twisted shell
That in immortal silence sleeps
Dreaming of her own melting hues,
Her golds, her ambers, and her blues,
Pierced with soft light the shallowing deeps.

Yeats finished *The Wanderings of Oisin* in Sligo in 1887. He now stayed with his uncle George Pollexfen, as well as with his grandparents who had left Merville, their large house on the outskirts of Sligo, for a house in the town. In March 1888 John Butler Yeats decided to rent a house in Blenheim Road, Bedford Park; the previous year he had moved the family from Dublin back to London, to 58 Eardley Crescent, where they were miserable and Mrs Yeats had her first stroke. She had another that year and from then on virtually opted out of life, dying in 1900. Money was very scarce indeed. Willie's small returns from magazine publication paid nearly all the household expenses, but food was short. It was an occasion for celebration when Lily Yeats was paid ten shillings a week for her work in May Morris's embroidery shop.

Out of homesickness for Sligo came 'The Lake Isle of Innisfree' in which Yeats thought he first achieved the rhythm of his own music. He was expanding his horizons. He admired the forcefulness of William Morris, whose Sunday evenings at Kelmscott House he frequented for a time; the energy and forthrightness of W. E. Henley, editor of the *Scots Observer*, also appealed to him, while Oscar Wilde's flowing conversation and social poise were to be envied and were a model, probably, for his own later deliberately achieved dignity. All three men were successful and contrasted with his father's apparent lack of willpower.

His own career, however, moved slowly. He had been published by Irish magazines while the family was in Dublin; now he had to make his way in London's literary life. Through O'Leary's contacts he had written for some American journals; Henley began to publish him in the *Scots Observer* and the *National Observer*; he contributed to the *Leisure Hour* and *The Bookman*. He edited *Fairy and Folk Tales of the Irish Peasantry* (1888), helped in editing *Poems and Ballads of Young Ireland* (1888), edited *Stories from Carleton* (1889), *Representative Irish Tales* (2 vols., 1891) and *Irish Fairy Tales* (1892). He wrote two tales, *John Sherman* and *Dhoya* (1891), and he began to edit Blake with his father's friend Edwin Ellis. Blake's emphasis upon contraries appealed to him, notably the proclamation in *The Marriage of Heaven and Hell* that 'Without Contraries is no progression. Attraction and Repulsion, Reason and Energy, Love and Hate, are necessary to Human Existence.' Yeats himself was pulled between his desire to believe and his questioning scepticism. Having founded the Hermetic Society in Dublin in 1888, he went on to join the Esoteric Section of the Theosophical Society in London, but was asked to leave two years later because of his desire for proof, his wish to experiment.

Into his life came Maud Gonne, in January 1889. She arrived at Blenheim Road with an introduction from John O'Leary and was all he had dreamed of; beautiful, tall and, though gentle, a ruthless revolutionary. The daughter of an English colonel, she liked the idea of violent action; she had been deeply moved by the plight of the poor in Ireland. Yeats had never thought 'to see in a living woman so great beauty'. It belonged to famous pictures, to poetry, to some legendary past: 'A complexion like the bloom of apples and yet face and body had the beauty of lineaments which Blake calls the highest beauty because it changes least from youth to age, and stature so great that she seemed of a divine race'.

What he called 'the troubling of his life' had begun. He was twenty-three, she twenty-two. He fell in love with her, but what could he do? He had not spoken of love 'and never meant to speak of love' and wondered 'what wife would she make . . . what share could she have in the life of a student?'. He offered to write a play for her, realizing she appreciated public talent, and began work on *The Countess Kathleen*. What could he do but offer his devotion, hoping that – some day – it might be requited? She stimulated his love poetry: it was devoted but defeatist in its melancholia. This mournful note dominated most of the poems in *The Countess Kathleen and Various Legends and Lyrics* (1892), for example, 'The Rose of the World' or 'The Rose of Battle' or 'The White Birds'. The Rose in the first Rose poems in this volume symbolized Maud Gonne, Ireland, intellectual beauty, and the Rosicrucian emblem of the Rose and the Cross, for, as he put it in 'To Ireland in the Coming Times', his

> . . . *rhymes more than their rhyming tell*
> *Of things discovered in the deep,*
> *Where only body's laid asleep.*

In 1890 he had joined the Hermetic Order of the Golden Dawn, attracted by its members' study of Rosicrucianism and ritual magic. The Society had been founded in 1888, its rituals amplifed by MacGregor Mathers (Samuel Liddel Mathers, 1854–1918, author of books on the Kabbala and the tarot cards, whom Yeats found impressive) into three ascending Orders. Yeats took it very seriously. In 1892 he wrote to John O'Leary, who, 'like his father, was apprehensive about the effect of this interest in magic on him', that he had decided 'four or five years ago' to make magic next to his poetry 'the most important pursuit of his life'. The mystical life, he went on, was the centre of what he did, all that he thought, all that he wrote. He had persuaded Maud Gonne to join the Order in 1891, though she soon left it, thinking its members a drab, mediocre, middle-class and very British lot. Yeats, however, remained and became a full member of the Second Order in 1893.

Yeats began to incorporate some of his new occult interests in his poetry in a cryptic way. His poetry was developing. In 1890 he founded, with Ernest Rhys (later to become famous as the editor of Dent's Everyman series), the Rhymers' Club, which met in a Fleet Street public house, The Cheshire Cheese. Here he met poets of the nineties, who included Lionel Johnson, Ernest Dowson, John Davidson, Arthur Symons and Oscar Wilde, who occasionally attended its meetings. Yeats believed he would learn his craft more thoroughly by discussing techniques with his fellow members.

Having sought to impress Maud Gonne by his writing of *The Countess Kathleen*, he also became active in his general ambition to awaken an awareness of past Irish writing and to stimulate new. Pursuing this aim with energy when the death of Parnell in 1891 seemed to offer a lull in Irish politics, and the hope that young Irish nationalists might now support Irish literature, Yeats founded Irish literary societies in London and in Dublin, planned the publication of Irish books, made speeches and wrote articles and reviews. The Irish Literary Renaissance came into being; he was immensely energetic in his efforts to create a sympathetic, supportive public for Irish writing.

In 1892 he published *The Celtic Twilight*, which contained some poems as well as essays largely about fairies or visionaries, people and places in Sligo. It was a volume without speculation or argument, possessed of an engaging simplicity, and it gave its name to the Irish literary movement as well as demonstrating Yeats's intellectual leadership.

Conversations with his fellow rhymers had made him feel less isolated – for he had experienced a sense of provincialism when he came to London. (This did not stop him constantly conveying his interest in Irish subject-matter, particularly in the supernatural, which gave him an unusually individual cachet in the literary world of London.) His respect for the learning of Lionel Johnson was succeeded by friendship with Arthur Symons, through whom he came to learn about the European symbolists, about the poets Verlaine and Mallarmé, the dramatist and poet Villiers de l'Isle Adam, and about the work of the Belgian playwright Maeterlinck. This interest was reflected in his own poetry. It had moved from the early descriptions of Irish places to epic material, the stories of Oisin, Fergus and Cuchulain; it developed from a limpid clarity to a mysterious elaboration in the 1890s. He kept ugliness out of it, distilling essences of beauty, mournful and spiritual, bringing into it echoes of magic rituals, mystical ideas. He had moved away from his early desire to write popular poetry in the poems of *The Wind Among the Reeds* (1899), which were intense, yet rarefied, delicately beautiful and weakly adjectival. This was the most elaborate development of his Celtic Twilight poetry.

This complex style (which was paralleled in his prose by 'The Autumn of the Body' and 'The Symbolism of Poetry') changed, gradually at first – as his next volume, *In the Seven Woods* (1903), indicates – through an alteration in the tone of his love poetry. For instance, 'Adam's Curse', probably written in 1901 after Maud Gonne had returned from political engagements in the United States, is an autobiographical memory, but also an account of the hard work that goes into making a poem, a line, seem spontaneous. (The story of the poem's inspiration is contained in Maud Gonne MacBride's autobiography, *A Servant of the Queen* (1938), pp. 328–30.) The old high way of love, however, had created through its frustrations a weariness of spirit – just as Yeats had noticed Maud Gonne's face was worn and thin. Her sister, 'That beautiful mild woman,' remarked that it was hard work being beautiful, a remark that triggered off this poem, which investigates the role of the poet in realistic rather than romantic terms:

We sat together at one summer's end,
That beautiful mild woman, your close friend,
And you and I, and talked of poetry.
I said, 'A line will take us hours maybe;
Yet if it does not seem a moment's thought,
Our stitching and unstitching has been naught.

Better go down upon your marrow-bones
And scrub a kitchen pavement, or break stones
Like an old pauper, in all kinds of weather;
For to articulate sweet sounds together
Is to work harder than all these, and yet
Be thought an idler by the noisy set
Of bankers, schoolmasters, and clergymen
The martyrs call the world'.

                  And thereupon
That beautiful mild woman for whose sake
There's many a one shall find out all heartache
On finding that her voice is sweet and low
Replied, 'To be born woman is to know –
Although they do not talk of it at school –
That we must labour to be beautiful.'

I said, 'It's certain there is no fine thing
Since Adam's fall but needs much labouring.
There have been lovers who thought love should be
So much compounded of high courtesy
That they would sigh and quote with learned looks
Precedents out of beautiful old books;
Yet now it seems an idle trade enough.'

We sat grown quiet at the name of love;
We saw the last embers of daylight die,
And in the trembling blue-green of the sky
A moon, worn as if it had been a shell
Washed by time's waters as they rose and fell

About the stars and broke in days and years.

I had a thought for no one's but your ears:
That you were beautiful, and that I strove
To love you in the old high way of love;
That it had all seemed happy, and yet we'd grown
As weary-hearted as that hollow moon.

In 1903 Maud Gonne married John MacBride, another revolutionary who had fought against the British in the Boer War. Yeats was surprised and deeply hurt, recording in his Diary how

My dear is angry that of late
I cry all base blood down
As if she had not taught me hate
By kisses to a clown.

Now he could merely record memories and old hopes, paying tribute to her great beauty – and his own celebration of it. In a superb series of poems (*The Green Helmet and Other Poems*, 1910) – 'Words', 'A Woman Homer Sung', 'No Second Troy' – he compares her to Helen of Troy. She is without blame, for she is, like Helen, beyond praise or comment. This volume indicates an almost complete transition of style, for here Yeats freely introduces topical affairs and his own views and beliefs, as well as recording the emptiness of his passion. The poems are simple, even flatly prosaic at times, for Yeats was preoccupied with 'theatre business, management of men'. He had become disillusioned with Irish politics and politicians largely as a result of his experiences with the Centenary Association, formed to mark the centenary of Wolfe Tone and the Revolution of 1798; he had been elected Chairman of the British and French branches and he had thought that the Dublin Committee could be turned into something like an Irish parliament. But he soon learned such a grandiose idea would not work in the world of Irish nationalist politics. He was disturbed by the riots which occurred in Dublin in 1897 on the occasion of Queen Victoria's Jubilee, and he left the I.R.B., disliking the violence that it bred.

He returned to a long-held ambition of creating an Irish theatre. He was helped in this by Lady Gregory, the widow of an Anglo-Irish landowner. He first visited her at Coole Park, her house in Co. Galway, in 1896, and the following year he spent the first of many summers there. It was an ideal place for him to recover his health from the incessant emotional and financial strains of previous years, and Lady Gregory provided him with an ideal ambience – he came to develop a belief in the virtues of both aristocratic and peasant life. Lady Gregory was a firm friend who urged him to give up journalism (and lent him money to enable him to do so), so that he could concentrate on his own creative writing. And, with her practicality and determination to aid him, he brought a national theatre into being.

In the first years they were helped by Edward Martyn, a neighbouring landowner, and George Moore the novelist, also a landowner, whose brief association with the Irish literary movement is told so well in his *Hail and Farewell*'s three volumes, *Ave, Salve, Vale*. The play Yeats had earlier written for Maud Gonne, *The Countess Kathleen*, was performed in 1899; other plays followed, and in 1902, when Martyn and Moore had dropped out of the movement, *Cathleen ni Houlihan*, the supreme expression of Yeats's early nationalism – and love – was performed with Maud Gonne in the title role. When the Abbey Theatre was established in 1904, Yeats became its production manager until 1910. The publication of his *Collected Works* in eight volumes in 1908 raised questions as to whether his poetic vein had been exhausted: 'All things', he wrote, 'can tempt me from this craft of verse.' He laid his

> curse on plays
> That have to be set up in fifty ways,
> On the day's war with every knave and dolt,
> Theatre business, management of men.

Yeats's role as manager of the Abbey was unselfish, for the theatre moved away from his own ideals of poetic drama towards the realistic work of other, younger dramatists. A further piece of unselfishness was his spirited defence of Synge's play, *The Playboy of the Western World*, in 1907. He had met Synge in Paris in 1896 and had urged on him the idea of visiting the Gaelic-speaking Aran islanders and making them the subject of his writing. Synge had become a co-director, with Lady Gregory and Yeats, of the limited company which replaced the previous national theatre in 1905; his work was unpopular with nationalist opinion, which regarded the *Playboy* as a slur on Irish manhood. Yeats courageously insisted on continuing to stage the play despite hostile audiences, but in the process he became even more disillusioned by his 'blind, bitter land'.

His next volume of poems, *Responsibilities* (1914), contains an entirely changed poetry, the antithesis of his early work, stripped of its decoration and mystery. In this he turned to savage satire and invective, defending great art against the philistines. Synge and Sir Hugh Lane (Lady Gregory's nephew) stand as his symbols of the artist and the enlightened patron. Lane's offering his collection of pictures as a gift to Dublin (on condition that a suitable gallery be built to house it) had not been properly appreciated, just as Synge's art had been despised by Dublin. Yeats began to praise the refinement and public-spiritedness of aristocratic life, drawing images from the great Renaissance patrons of Italy (after the row over the *Playboy* he had visited Italy with Lady Gregory and her son Robert and was immensely stimulated by seeing Urbino and Ferrara in particular), and he also veered to the other extreme, a gusty enjoyment of coarseness in the poems he wrote about beggars. He repudiated all the Celtic Twilight's embroideries out of old mythologies in 'A Coat'; he recorded his disillusionment with the realities of Ireland in 'The Fisherman'; and he inveighed against her ingratitude to her benefactors in 'To A Shade'. Behind all this can be discerned the ground swell of his frustrated love for Maud Gonne. Because of a barren passion he cannot offer his ancestors children to continue the family line, and yet his constant praise of her beauty and her love of the people whom he had begun to distrust continues; it spills over into poems published some years later in *The Wild Swans at Coole* (1919), such as 'Her Praise', 'His Phoenix' and 'The People'.

In the years leading up to the First World War Yeats moved into a middle age that had much achievement, into a period when he learned to hide his innate shyness behind a somewhat mannered mask. He had moved out of the family house in 1896 and taken rooms in Woburn Buildings – partially because, for a year, he had an affair with Mrs Shakespear; they had, he recorded in his unpublished autobiography, many days of happiness. The unrequited love for Maud Gonne, however, was only briefly in abeyance. Olivia Shakespear realized this. 'There is someone else in your heart,' she said. 'It was the breaking between us for many years.'

In 1898 he and Maud Gonne had experienced a 'spiritual marriage' which ended when she married MacBride. After that Yeats had an affair with Florence Farr, the independent young woman who had acted in his play *The Land of Heart's Desire*, and, as Aleel the poet, in *The Countess Kathleen*. His friendship with Olivia Shakespear was resumed. And the spiritual marriage with Maud was renewed in 1908, balanced by a relationship, largely physical, with Mabel Dickinson, which ended stormily in 1913. Yeats had many friends in England, among them the lively young iconoclast Ezra Pound, who acted as his secretary in the winter of 1913. Pound married Olivia Shakespear's daughter Dorothy, and Yeats spent some of the winters of 1915 and 1916 with them at Stone Cottage in Sussex.

Here he developed an interest in a new kind of play. Tired of the Abbey audiences' reactions to heroic plays, their preference for realistic cottage comedies, he wrote plays for smaller, select audiences, his *Plays for Dancers*, which were stimulated by Ezra

Pound's work on Ernest Fenollosa's translations of Japanese
Nōh plays. He received a Civil List pension of £150 a year in
1910; he refused the offer of a knighthood in 1915. He had made
enough money by his lecture tours in America (in 1903-4, 1911
and 1914) to pay Lady Gregory what he owed her, and he was
able to support his father, who had gone to New York in 1907,
by selling manuscripts of his work to John Quinn, the Irish-
American lawyer who was a generous patron of Irish writers
and artists. It seemed time to begin writing his autobiography
and he finished the first part of it in 1914, imposing a pattern on
selected experiences.

In the opening years of the century he had been involved in
quarrels with the Order of the Golden Dawn, but later he
developed a strong interest in spiritualism, becoming an associ-
ate member of the Society for Psychical Research, and inves-
tigating the automatic writing of Elizabeth Radcliffe. He
thought the First World War destructive, 'bloody frivolity':

> We have no gift to set a statesman right;
> He has had enough of meddling who can please
> A young girl in the indolence of her youth,
> Or an old man upon a winter's night.

The Easter Rising of 1916 took him completely by surprise. The
revolutionaries he had come to despise attained heroic stature
and it seemed to him that a terrible beauty was born. Maud
Gonne's husband (from whom she had been separated) was one
of the sixteen leaders executed, and Yeats went to France and
proposed to her again, but, as in the past, she refused him. Then
he asked her permission to propose to her daughter Iseult
(whose father was Lucien Millevoye, by whom Maud Gonne
had had an earlier child, a son Georges, who died in 1891). He
had written several poems to Iseult in preceding years. She
refused him, and in October 1917 he married Georgie Hyde
Lees, whom he had known for some years.

His marriage made his life 'serene and full of order', and it also provided the starting-point for an altogether unexpected conjunction of his romantic and his realistic strains of poetry. Mrs Yeats attempted automatic writing because Yeats was unhappy at the beginning of their marriage (through concern over Iseult Gonne; later poems 'Two Songs of a Fool', 'To a Young Beauty', 'Michael Robartes and the Dancer', and 'Owen Aherne and his Dancers', illustrate this), and to her surprise odd sentences were produced on a subject of which she knew nothing. Yeats was excited and stimulated, and spent hours every day on the decipherment of this automatic script; he seemed to be able to believe, even though only temporarily, in the system thus built up, which he published privately under the title of *A Vision* in 1926, and later, through Macmillans, in 1937.

This work is 'a system of symbolism', as Yeats explained in *A Packet for Ezra Pound* (1934), which deals with various types of human personality, with the 'gyres' of historical change and with the supernatural. It provided, in part, a structure for Yeats's thought, for the ideas he had been assimilating from his unusual reading. He had read deeply in Swedenborg and Bochme, in Stanislaus de Guaita and Joachim of Fiore, in Henry More and, of course, in Plato and the Neoplatonists. Creating *A Vision* gave him confidence and strength so that he wrote out of all the fullness of his interests, finding in himself and his thought a sufficient subject for poetry. The first poems relating to *A Vision* appeared in *The Wild Swans at Coole* (1919) – 'The Phases of the Moon' and 'Hic and Ille' and, perhaps the most impressive of them, 'The Second Coming' in *Michael Robartes and the Dancer* (1921).

These two volumes show the reblossoming of his poetry after the cold winter rages of *Responsibilities*. In such poems as 'In Memory of Major Robert Gregory', 'Easter 1916' and 'A Prayer for My Daughter', Yeats is able to write with authority, to blend his appreciation of beauty with a sense of the tragic rather than the pathetic elements of life, to give a significance to the ordinary events of life which his earlier poetry avoided, and to attain in the process a personal means of achieving public speech in poetry.

His life had blossomed too. The erstwhile revolutionary turned cynic now became a Senator of the Irish Free State, and an active, constructive one at that; all the Senators, himself included, seemed to him like 'coral insects with some design in our heads of the ultimate island'. He spoke frequently and made his main contribution as Chairman of the Commission on Coinage (his Report is a model of its kind), though he regarded all matters connected with art or literature as coming within his province, and on these he was heard with respect. 'Among School Children' gives us a brief vignette of him as a 'sixty-year-old smiling public man'.

The award of the Nobel Prize for Literature (1923) gave public recognition to his work. He had bought Ballylee Castle for £35 in 1917, and called it Thoor Ballylee, from the Irish *tur*, a tower. It was a medieval Norman tower in Co. Galway, which he and his wife set about restoring and where they now lived for part of the year. It was the first house he owned and it provided him with a visible symbol of the Anglo-Irish tradition which he began to explore excitedly. He read Swift, Goldsmith, Berkeley and Burke and saw himself as an inheritor of their traditions, where plain speech and clarity were the basis of rhetoric. The Yeats line was secure now, for the birth of his daughter was followed by that of a son. With this flowering of his life when opposites seemed conjoined – poet and Nobel Prize-winner, man of action and Senator – came the maturity of his style. He uses a symbolism which is direct in its speech, recording the richness of his life as well as its bitterness. As his youthful ambitions were realized he saw the paradoxes of life. Irish freedom was achieved, but the glorious great houses were burnt down. Wisdom might perhaps compensate him for the loss of youth; but as his body aged his muse grew younger, 'the real man, the imagination which liveth for ever'. As a result he wrote 'The Tower' and 'Sailing to Byzantium', passionate poems of tension between the sensual and the spiritual, their unity arising out of his own complexity.

This warring of the antinomies continued in *The Winding Stair* (1933) in 'A Dialogue of Self and Soul' with its triumphant pagan affirmation of belief in human life echoed later in 'Vacillation'. The contrast lay in the passing of glory. Coole Park (the significance of which as a focal point of Irish culture he celebrated in 'Coole Park, 1929') had been sold to the Forestry Commission with the understanding that Lady Gregory should rent the house and part of the demesne until her death. Now in 'Coole Park and Ballylee, 1931' he realizes Lady Gregory is dying, and with her the dignity and loveliness of a house which symbolized the inherited yet living glory of an aristocratic life.

Yeats himself suffered from severe illness in the winter of 1927-28, evidenced by 'At Algeciras – a Meditation upon Death', but the spring of 1929 was an exuberantly creative period when he wrote several of the Crazy Jane poems and the other lyrics which appeared in *Words for Music Perhaps* (1931).

A Full Moon in March (1935) contained 'Supernatural Songs', written out of a Donne-like delight in obscure thought condensed into arresting phrase. He was working with Shri Purohit Swami on a translation of the Upanishads and compiling *The Oxford Book of Modern Verse* when he had another serious illness; but his poetry continued to develop and he prayed for 'an old man's frenzy' in order to remake himself, to remodel his personality. He wrote out of rage and lust ('Why should not old men be mad?' asks one poem), but also out of a sense of simplicity and grandeur.

His moods of unity could produce in *Last Poems* such Olympian poetry as 'The Municipal Gallery Revisited', or 'Beautiful Lofty Things', in which he praised his friends generously and warmly, concentrating brilliantly upon aspects of their work or lives, which he caught in terse unforgettable phrases. 'The Gyres' and 'The Statues' reverted to the material of *A Vision*, contemplating the cycles of historical change and the power of abstract thought, while 'The Circus Animals' Desertion' analysed his career with devastating honesty.

Filled with energy, he fought death to the end, but in 'The Man and the Echo' came to realize that all he knew was that he did not know what death brought. He hated old age; he called upon his ancestors to judge what he had done in 'Are you Content?'; and he wrote 'Under Ben Bulben' as his own epitaph and elegy, with all its passionate affirmations of what made up, for him, the indomitable qualities of the Irish, qualities which ensured the success of his long struggle to make himself a great and, always, an Irish poet. He died in France and was buried in the cemetery at Roquebrune in January 1939. His body was brought to Ireland and interred at Drumcliff in September 1948.

From *CROSSWAYS*

THE SONG OF THE HAPPY SHEPHERD

THE woods of Arcady are dead,
And over is their antique joy;
Of old the world on dreaming fed;
Grey Truth is now her painted toy;
Yet still she turns her restless head:
But O, sick children of the world,
Of all the many changing things
In dreary dancing past us whirled,
To the cracked tune that Chronos sings,
Words alone are certain good.
Where are now the warring kings,
Word be-mockers? — By the Rood,
Where are now the warring kings?
An idle word is now their glory,
By the stammering schoolboy said,
Reading some entangled story:
The kings of the old time are dead;
The wandering earth herself may be
Only a sudden flaming word,
In clanging space a moment heard,
Troubling the endless reverie.

Then nowise worship dusty deeds,
Nor seek, for this is also sooth,
To hunger fiercely after truth,
Lest all thy toiling only breeds
New dreams, new dreams; there is no truth

Saving in thine own heart. Seek, then,
No learning from the starry men,
Who follow with the optic glass
The whirling ways of stars that pass —
Seek, then, for this is also sooth,
No word of theirs — the cold star-bane
Has cloven and rent their hearts in twain,
And dead is all their human truth.
Go gather by the humming sea
Some twisted, echo-harbouring shell,
And to its lips thy story tell,
And they thy comforters will be,
Rewording in melodious guile
Thy fretful words a little while,
Till they shall singing fade in ruth
And die a pearly brotherhood;
For words alone are certain good:
Sing, then, for this is also sooth.

I must be gone: there is a grave
Where daffodil and lily wave,
And I would please the hapless faun,
Buried under the sleepy ground,
With mirthful songs before the dawn.
His shouting days with mirth were crowned;
And still I dream he treads the lawn,
Walking ghostly in the dew,
Pierced by my glad singing through,
My songs of old earth's dreamy youth:
But ah! she dreams not now; dream thou!
For fair are poppies on the brow:
Dream, dream, for this is also sooth.

THE SAD SHEPHERD

THERE was a man whom Sorrow named his friend,
And he, of his high comrade Sorrow dreaming,
Went walking with slow steps along the gleaming
And humming sands, where windy surges wend:
And he called loudly to the stars to bend
From their pale thrones and comfort him, but they
Among themselves laugh on and sing alway:
And then the man whom Sorrow named his friend
Cried out, *Dim sea, hear my most piteous story!*
The sea swept on and cried her old cry still,
Rolling along in dreams from hill to hill.
He fled the persecution of her glory
And, in a far-off, gentle valley stopping,
Cried all his story to the dewdrops glistening.
But naught they heard, for they are always listening,
The dewdrops, for the sound of their own dropping.
And then the man whom Sorrow named his friend
Sought once again the shore, and found a shell,
And thought, *I will my heavy story tell*
Till my own words, re-echoing, shall send
Their sadness through a hollow, pearly heart;
And my own tale again for me shall sing,
And my own whispering words be comforting,
And lo! my ancient burden may depart.
Then he sang softly nigh the pearly rim;
But the sad dweller by the sea-ways lone
Changed all he sang to inarticulate moan
Among her wildering whirls, forgetting him.

EPHEMERA

'YOUR eyes that once were never weary of mine
Are bowed in sorrow under pendulous lids,
Because our love is waning.'
                              And then she:
'Although our love is waning, let us stand
By the lone border of the lake once more,
Together in that hour of gentleness
When the poor tired child, Passion, falls asleep.
How far away the stars seem, and how far
Is our first kiss, and ah, how old my heart!'

Pensive they paced along the faded leaves,
While slowly he whose hand held hers replied:
'Passion has often worn our wandering hearts.'

The woods were round them, and the yellow leaves
Fell like faint meteors in the gloom, and once
A rabbit old and lame limped down the path;
Autumn was over him: and now they stood
On the lone border of the lake once more:
Turning, he saw that she had thrust dead leaves
Gathered in silence, dewy as her eyes,
In bosom and hair.
                      'Ah, do not mourn,' he said,
'That we are tired, for other loves await us;
Hate on and love through unrepining hours.
Before us lies eternity; our souls
Are love, and a continual farewell.'

THE STOLEN CHILD

WHERE dips the rocky highland
Of Sleuth Wood in the lake,
There lies a leafy island
Where flapping herons wake
The drowsy water-rats;
There we've hid our faery vats,
Full of berries
And of reddest stolen cherries.
Come away, O human child!
To the waters and the wild
With a faery, hand in hand,
For the world's more full of weeping than you
can understand.

Where the wave of moonlight glosses
The dim grey sands with light,
Far off by furthest Rosses
We foot it all the night,
Weaving olden dances,
Mingling hands and mingling glances
Till the moon has taken flight;
To and fro we leap
And chase the frothy bubbles,
While the world is full of troubles
And is anxious in its sleep.
Come away, O human child!
To the waters and the wild
With a faery, hand in hand,
For the world's more full of weeping than you
can understand.

Where the wandering water gushes
From the hills above Glen-Car,
In pools among the rushes
That scarce could bathe a star,
We seek for slumbering trout
And whispering in their ears
Give them unquiet dreams;
Leaning softly out
From ferns that drop their tears
Over the young streams.
Come away, O human child!
To the waters and the wild
With a faery, hand in hand,
For the world's more full of weeping than you
     can understand.

Away with us he's going,
The solemn-eyed:
He'll hear no more the lowing
Of the calves on the warm hillside
Or the kettle on the hob
Sing peace into his breast,
Or see the brown mice bob
Round and round the oatmeal-chest.
For he comes, the human child,
To the waters and the wild
With a faery, hand in hand,
From a world more full of weeping than he
     can understand.

DOWN BY THE SALLEY GARDENS

Down by the salley gardens my love and I did meet;
She passed the salley gardens with little snow-white feet.
She bid me take love easy, as the leaves grow on the tree;
But I, being young and foolish, with her would not agree.

In a field by the river my love and I did stand,
And on my leaning shoulder she laid her snow-white hand.
She bid me take life easy, as the grass grows on the weirs;
But I was young and foolish, and now am full of tears.

THE BALLAD OF MOLL MAGEE

Come round me, little childer;
There, don't fling stones at me
Because I mutter as I go;
But pity Moll Magee.

My man was a poor fisher
With shore lines in the say;
My work was saltin' herrings
The whole of the long day.

And sometimes from the saltin' shed
I scarce could drag my feet,
Under the blessed moonlight,
Along the pebbly street.

I'd always been but weakly,
And my baby was just born;
A neighbour minded her by day,
I minded her till morn.

I lay upon my baby;
Ye little childer dear,
I looked on my cold baby
When the morn grew frosty and clear.

A weary woman sleeps so hard!
My man grew red and pale,
And gave me money, and bade me go
To my own place, Kinsale.

He drove me out and shut the door,
And gave his curse to me;
I went away in silence,
No neighbour could I see.

The windows and the doors were shut,
One star shone faint and green,
The little straws were turnin' round
Across the bare boreen.

I went away in silence:
Beyond old Martin's byre
I saw a kindly neighbour
Blowin' her mornin' fire.

She drew from me my story —
My money's all used up,
And still, with pityin', scornin' eye,
She gives me bite and sup.

She says my man will surely come
And fetch me home agin;
But always, as I'm movin' round,
Without doors or within,

Pilin' the wood or pilin' the turf,
Or goin' to the well,
I'm thinkin' of my baby
And keenin' to mysel'.

And sometimes I am sure she knows
When, openin' wide His door,
God lights the stars, His candles,
And looks upon the poor.

So now, ye little childer,
Ye won't fling stones at me;
But gather with your shinin' looks
And pity Moll Magee.

From *THE ROSE*

TO THE ROSE UPON THE ROOD OF TIME

RED Rose, proud Rose, sad Rose of all my days!
Come near me, while I sing the ancient ways:
Cuchulain battling with the bitter tide;
The Druid, grey, wood-nurtured, quiet-eyed,
Who cast round Fergus dreams, and ruin untold;
And thine own sadness, whereof stars, grown old
In dancing silver-sandalled on the sea,
Sing in their high and lonely melody.
Come near, that no more blinded by man's fate,
I find under the boughs of love and hate,
In all poor foolish things that live a day,
Eternal beauty wandering on her way.

Come near, come near, come near — Ah, leave me still
A little space for the rose-breath to fill!
Lest I no more hear common things that crave;
The weak worm hiding down in its small cave,
The field-mouse running by me in the grass,
And heavy mortal hopes that toil and pass;
But seek alone to hear the strange things said
By God to the bright hearts of those long dead,
And learn to chaunt a tongue men do not know.
Come near; I would, before my time to go,
Sing of old Eire and the ancient ways:
Red Rose, proud Rose, sad Rose of all my days.

FERGUS AND THE DRUID

Fergus. This whole day have I followed in the rocks,
  And you have changed and flowed from shape to shape,
  First as a raven on whose ancient wings
  Scarcely a feather lingered, then you seemed
  A weasel moving on from stone to stone,
  And now at last you wear a human shape,
  A thin grey man half lost in gathering night.

Druid. What would you, king of the proud Red Branch kings?

Fergus. This would I say, most wise of living souls:
  Young subtle Conchubar sat close by me
  When I gave judgment, and his words were wise,
  And what to me was burden without end,
  To him seemed easy, so I laid the crown
  Upon his head to cast away my sorrow.

Druid. What would you, king of the proud Red Branch kings?

Fergus. A king and proud! and that is my despair.
  I feast amid my people on the hill,
  And pace the woods, and drive my chariot-wheels
  In the white border of the murmuring sea;
  And still I feel the crown upon my head.

Druid. What would you, Fergus?

Fergus.   Be no more a king
  But learn the dreaming wisdom that is yours.

Druid. Look on my thin grey hair and hollow cheeks
   And on these hands that may not lift the sword,
   This body trembling like a wind-blown reed.
   No woman's loved me, no man sought my help.

Fergus. A king is but a foolish labourer
   Who wastes his blood to be another's dream.

Druid. Take, if you must, this little bag of dreams;
   Unloose the cord, and they will wrap you round.

Fergus. I see my life go drifting like a river
   From change to change; I have been many things —
   A green drop in the surge, a gleam of light
   Upon a sword, a fir-tree on a hill,
   An old slave grinding at a heavy quern,
   A king sitting upon a chair of gold —
   And all these things were wonderful and great;
   But now I have grown nothing, knowing all.
   Ah! Druid, Druid, how great webs of sorrow
   Lay hidden in the small slate-coloured thing!

CUCHULAIN'S FIGHT WITH THE SEA

A MAN came slowly from the setting sun,
To Emer, raddling raiment in her dun,
And said, 'I am that swineherd whom you bid
Go watch the road between the wood and tide,
But now I have no need to watch it more.'

Then Emer cast the web upon the floor,
And raising arms all raddled with the dye,
Parted her lips with a loud sudden cry.

That swineherd stared upon her face and said,
'No man alive, no man among the dead,
Has won the gold his cars of battle bring.'

'But if your master comes home triumphing
Why must you blench and shake from foot to crown?'

Thereon he shook the more and cast him down
Upon the web-heaped floor, and cried his word:
'With him is one sweet-throated like a bird.'

'You dare me to my face,' and thereupon
She smote with raddled fist, and where her son
Herded the cattle came with stumbling feet,
And cried with angry voice, 'It is not meet
To idle life away, a common herd.'

'I have long waited, mother, for that word:
But wherefore now?'

                   'There is a man to die;
You have the heaviest arm under the sky.'

'Whether under its daylight or its stars
My father stands amid his battle-cars.'

'But you have grown to be the taller man.'

'Yet somewhere under starlight or the sun
My father stands.'

                 'Aged, worn out with wars
On foot, on horseback or in battle-cars.'

'I only ask what way my journey lies,
For He who made you bitter made you wise.'

'The Red Branch camp in a great company
Between wood's rim and the horses of the sea.
Go there, and light a camp-fire at wood's rim;
But tell your name and lineage to him
Whose blade compels, and wait till they have found
Some feasting man that the same oath has bound.'

Among those feasting men Cuchulain dwelt,
And his young sweetheart close beside him knelt,
Stared on the mournful wonder of his eyes,
Even as Spring upon the ancient skies,
And pondered on the glory of his days;
And all around the harp-string told his praise,
And Conchubar, the Red Branch king of kings,
With his own fingers touched the brazen strings.

At last Cuchulain spake, 'Some man has made
His evening fire amid the leafy shade.
I have often heard him singing to and fro,
I have often heard the sweet sound of his bow.
Seek out what man he is.'

                              One went and came.
'He bade me let all know he gives his name
At the sword-point, and waits till we have found
Some feasting man that the same oath has bound.'

Cuchulain cried, 'I am the only man
Of all this host so bound from childhood on.'

After short fighting in the leafy shade,
He spake to the young man, 'Is there no maid
Who loves you, no white arms to wrap you round,
Or do you long for the dim sleepy ground,
That you have come and dared me to my face?'

'The dooms of men are in God's hidden place.'

'Your head a while seemed like a woman's head
That I loved once.'

                    Again the fighting sped,
But now the war-rage in Cuchulain woke,
And through that new blade's guard the old blade broke,
And pierced him.

                  'Speak before your breath is done.'

'Cuchulain I, mighty Cuchulain's son.'

'I put you from your pain. I can no more.'

While day its burden on to evening bore,
With head bowed on his knees Cuchulain stayed;
Then Conchubar sent that sweet-throated maid,
And she, to win him, his grey hair caressed;
In vain her arms, in vain her soft white breast.
Then Conchubar, the subtlest of all men,
Ranking his Druids round him ten by ten,
Spake thus: 'Cuchulain will dwell there and brood
For three days more in dreadful quietude,
And then arise, and raving slay us all.
Chaunt in his ear delusions magical,
That he may fight the horses of the sea.'
The Druids took them to their mystery,
And chaunted for three days.

                    Cuchulain stirred,
Stared on the horses of the sea, and heard
The cars of battle and his own name cried;
And fought with the invulnerable tide.

THE LAKE ISLE OF INNISFREE

I WILL arise and go now, and go to Innisfree,
And a small cabin build there, of clay and wattles made:
Nine bean-rows will I have there, a hive for the honey-bee,
And live alone in the bee-loud glade.

And I shall have some peace there, for peace comes dropping
    slow,
Dropping from the veils of the morning to where the cricket
    sings;
There midnight's all a glimmer, and noon a purple glow,
And evening full of the linnet's wings.

I will arise and go now, for always night and day
I hear lake water lapping with low sounds by the shore;
While I stand on the roadway, or on the pavements grey,
I hear it in the deep heart's core.

THE PITY OF LOVE

A PITY beyond all telling
Is hid in the heart of love:
The folk who are buying and selling,
The clouds on their journey above,
The cold wet winds ever blowing,
And the shadowy hazel grove
Where mouse-grey waters are flowing,
Threaten the head that I love.

THE SORROW OF LOVE

THE brawling of a sparrow in the eaves,
The brilliant moon and all the milky sky,
And all that famous harmony of leaves,
Had blotted out man's image and his cry.

A girl arose that had red mournful lips
And seemed the greatness of the world in tears,
Doomed like Odysseus and the labouring ships
And proud as Priam murdered with his peers;

Arose, and on the instant clamorous eaves,
A climbing moon upon an empty sky,
And all that lamentation of the leaves,
Could but compose man's image and his cry.

WHEN YOU ARE OLD

WHEN you are old and grey and full of sleep,
And nodding by the fire, take down this book,
And slowly read, and dream of the soft look
Your eyes had once, and of their shadows deep;

How many loved your moments of glad grace,
And loved your beauty with love false or true,
But one man loved the pilgrim soul in you,
And loved the sorrows of your changing face;

And bending down beside the glowing bars,
Murmur, a little sadly, how Love fled
And paced upon the mountains overhead
And hid his face amid a crowd of stars.

THE WHITE BIRDS

I would that we were, my beloved, white birds on the foam
   of the sea!
We tire of the flame of the meteor, before it can fade and
   flee;
And the flame of the blue star of twilight, hung low on the
   rim of the sky,
Has awaked in our hearts, my beloved, a sadness that may not
   die.

A weariness comes from those dreamers, dew-dabbled, the
   lily and rose;
Ah, dream not of them, my beloved, the flame of the meteor
   that goes,
Or the flame of the blue star that lingers hung low in the fall
   of the dew:
For I would we were changed to white birds on the wandering
   foam: I and you!

I am haunted by numberless islands, and many a Danaan
   shore,
Where Time would surely forget us, and Sorrow come near
   us no more;
Soon far from the rose and the lily and fret of the flames would
   we be,
Were we only white birds, my beloved, buoyed out on the
   foam of the sea!

THE MAN WHO DREAMED OF FAERYLAND

HE stood among a crowd at Dromahair;
His heart hung all upon a silken dress,
And he had known at last some tenderness,
Before earth took him to her stony care;
But when a man poured fish into a pile,
It seemed they raised their little silver heads,
And sang what gold morning or evening sheds
Upon a woven world-forgotten isle
Where people love beside the ravelled seas;
That Time can never mar a lover's vows
Under that woven changeless roof of boughs:
The singing shook him out of his new ease.

He wandered by the sands of Lissadell;
His mind ran all on money cares and fears,
And he had known at last some prudent years
Before they heaped his grave under the hill;
But while he passed before a plashy place,
A lug-worm with its grey and muddy mouth
Sang that somewhere to north or west or south
There dwelt a gay, exulting, gentle race
Under the golden or the silver skies;
That if a dancer stayed his hungry foot
It seemed the sun and moon were in the fruit:
And at that singing he was no more wise.

He mused beside the well of Scanavin,
He mused upon his mockers: without fail
His sudden vengeance were a country tale,
When earthy night had drunk his body in;

But one small knot-grass growing by the pool
Sang where — unnecessary cruel voice —
Old silence bids its chosen race rejoice,
Whatever ravelled waters rise and fall
Or stormy silver fret the gold of day,
And midnight there enfold them like a fleece
And lover there by lover be at peace.
The tale drove his fine angry mood away.

He slept under the hill of Lugnagall;
And might have known at last unhaunted sleep
Under that cold and vapour-turbaned steep,
Now that the earth had taken man and all:
Did not the worms that spired about his bones
Proclaim with that unwearied, reedy cry
That God has laid His fingers on the sky,
That from those fingers glittering summer runs
Upon the dancer by the dreamless wave.
Why should those lovers that no lovers miss
Dream, until God burn Nature with a kiss?
The man has found no comfort in the grave.

THE TWO TREES

BELOVED, gaze in thine own heart,
The holy tree is growing there;
From joy the holy branches start,
And all the trembling flowers they bear.
The changing colours of its fruit
Have dowered the stars with merry light;
The surety of its hidden root
Has planted quiet in the night;

The shaking of its leafy head
Has given the waves their melody,
And made my lips and music wed,
Murmuring a wizard song for thee.
There the Loves a circle go,
The flaming circle of our days,
Gyring, spiring to and fro
In those great ignorant leafy ways;
Remembering all that shaken hair
And how the wingèd sandals dart,
Thine eyes grow full of tender care:
Beloved, gaze in thine own heart.

Gaze no more in the bitter glass
The demons, with their subtle guile,
Lift up before us when they pass,
Or only gaze a little while;
For there a fatal image grows
That the stormy night receives,
Roots half hidden under snows,
Broken boughs and blackened leaves.
For all things turn to barrenness
In the dim glass the demons hold,
The glass of outer weariness,
Made when God slept in times of old.
There, through the broken branches, go
The ravens of unresting thought;
Flying, crying, to and fro,
Cruel claw and hungry throat,
Or else they stand and sniff the wind,
And shake their ragged wings; alas!
Thy tender eyes grow all unkind:
Gaze no more in the bitter glass.

TO IRELAND IN THE COMING TIMES

KNOW, that I would accounted be
True brother of a company
That sang, to sweeten Ireland's wrong,
Ballad and story, rann and song;
Nor be I any less of them,
Because the red-rose-bordered hem
Of her, whose history began
Before God made the angelic clan,
Trails all about the written page.
When Time began to rant and rage
The measure of her flying feet
Made Ireland's heart begin to beat;
And Time bade all his candles flare
To light a measure here and there;
And may the thoughts of Ireland brood
Upon a measured quietude.

Nor may I less be counted one
With Davis, Mangan, Ferguson,
Because, to him who ponders well,
My rhymes more than their rhyming tell
Of things discovered in the deep,
Where only body's laid asleep.
For the elemental creatures go
About my table to and fro,
That hurry from unmeasured mind
To rant and rage in flood and wind,
Yet he who treads in measured ways
May surely barter gaze for gaze.
Man ever journeys on with them
After the red-rose-bordered hem.

Ah, faeries, dancing under the moon,
A Druid land, a Druid tune!

While still I may, I write for you
The love I lived, the dream I knew.
From our birthday, until we die,
Is but the winking of an eye;
And we, our singing and our love,
What measurer Time has lit above,
And all benighted things that go
About my table to and fro,
Are passing on to where may be,
In truth's consuming ecstasy,
No place for love and dream at all;
For God goes by with white footfall.
I cast my heart into my rhymes,
That you, in the dim coming times,
May know how my heart went with them
After the red-rose-bordered hem.

From *THE WIND AMONG THE REEDS*

THE HOSTING OF THE SIDHE

THE host is riding from Knocknarea
And over the grave of Clooth-na-Bare;
Caoilte tossing his burning hair,
And Niamh calling *Away, come away:*
Empty your heart of its mortal dream.
The winds awaken, the leaves whirl round,
Our cheeks are pale, our hair is unbound,
Our breasts are heaving, our eyes are agleam,
Our arms are waving, our lips are apart;
And if any gaze on our rushing band,
We come between him and the deed of his hand,
We come between him and the hope of his heart.
The host is rushing 'twixt night and day,
And where is there hope or deed as fair?
Caoilte tossing his burning hair,
And Niamh calling *Away, come away.*

THE LOVER TELLS OF THE ROSE IN HIS HEART

ALL things uncomely and broken, all things worn out and old,
The cry of a child by the roadway, the creak of a lumbering cart,
The heavy steps of the ploughman, splashing the wintry mould,
Are wronging your image that blossoms a rose in the deeps of my heart.

The wrong of unshapely things is a wrong too great to be
    told;
I hunger to build them anew and sit on a green knoll apart,
With the earth and the sky and the water, re-made, like a
    casket of gold
For my dreams of your image that blossoms a rose in the
    deeps of my heart.

THE HOST OF THE AIR

O'DRISCOLL drove with a song
The wild duck and the drake
From the tall and the tufted reeds
Of the drear Hart Lake.

And he saw how the reeds grew dark
At the coming of night-tide,
And dreamed of the long dim hair
Of Bridget his bride.

He heard while he sang and dreamed
A piper piping away,
And never was piping so sad,
And never was piping so gay.

And he saw young men and young girls
Who danced on a level place,
And Bridget his bride among them,
With a sad and a gay face.

The dancers crowded about him
And many a sweet thing said,
And a young man brought him red wine
And a young girl white bread.

But Bridget drew him by the sleeve
Away from the merry bands,
To old men playing at cards
With a twinkling of ancient hands.

The bread and the wine had a doom,
For these were the host of the air;
He sat and played in a dream
Of her long dim hair.

He played with the merry old men
And thought not of evil chance.
Until one bore Bridget his bride
Away from the merry dance.

He bore her away in his arms,
The handsomest young man there,
And his neck and his breast and his arms
Were drowned in her long dim hair.

O'Driscoll scattered the cards
And out of his dream awoke:
Old men and young men and young girls
Were gone like a drifting smoke;

But he heard high up in the air
A piper piping away,
And never was piping so sad,
And never was piping so gay.

THE UNAPPEASABLE HOST

THE Danaan children laugh, in cradles of wrought gold,
And clap their hands together, and half close their eyes,
For they will ride the North when the ger-eagle flies,
With heavy whitening wings, and a heart fallen cold:
I kiss my wailing child and press it to my breast,
And hear the narrow graves calling my child and me.
Desolate winds that cry over the wandering sea;
Desolate winds that hover in the flaming West;
Desolate winds that beat the doors of Heaven, and beat
The doors of Hell and blow there many a whimpering ghost;
O heart the winds have shaken, the unappeasable host
Is comelier than candles at Mother Mary's feet.

THE SONG OF WANDERING AENGUS

I WENT out to the hazel wood,
Because a fire was in my head,
And cut and peeled a hazel wand,
And hooked a berry to a thread;
And when white moths were on the wing,
And moth-like stars were flickering out,
I dropped the berry in a stream
And caught a little silver trout.

When I had laid it on the floor
I went to blow the fire aflame,
But something rustled on the floor,
And some one called me by my name:
It had become a glimmering girl

With apple blossom in her hair
Who called me by my name and ran
And faded through the brightening air.

Though I am old with wandering
Through hollow lands and hilly lands,
I will find out where she has gone,
And kiss her lips and take her hands;
And walk among long dappled grass,
And pluck till time and times are done
The silver apples of the moon,
The golden apples of the sun.

HE MOURNS FOR THE CHANGE THAT HAS COME
    UPON HIM AND HIS BELOVED, AND LONGS
    FOR THE END OF THE WORLD

Do you not hear me calling, white deer with no horns?
I have been changed to a hound with one red ear;
I have been in the Path of Stones and the Wood of Thorns,
For somebody hid hatred and hope and desire and fear
Under my feet that they follow you night and day.
A man with a hazel wand came without sound;
He changed me suddenly; I was looking another way;
And now my calling is but the calling of a hound;
And Time and Birth and Change are hurrying by.
I would that the Boar without bristles had come from the
    West
And had rooted the sun and moon and stars out of the sky
And lay in the darkness, grunting, and turning to his rest.

HE BIDS HIS BELOVED BE AT PEACE

I HEAR the Shadowy Horses, their long manes a-shake,
Their hoofs heavy with tumult, their eyes glimmering white;
The North unfolds above them clinging, creeping night,
The East her hidden joy before the morning break,
The West weeps in pale dew and sighs passing away,
The South is pouring down roses of crimson fire:
O vanity of Sleep, Hope, Dream, endless Desire,
The Horses of Disaster plunge in the heavy clay:
Beloved, let your eyes half close, and your heart beat
Over my heart, and your hair fall over my breast,
Drowning love's lonely hour in deep twilight of rest,
And hiding their tossing manes and their tumultuous feet.

HE REMEMBERS FORGOTTEN BEAUTY

WHEN my arms wrap you round I press
My heart upon the loveliness
That has long faded from the world;
The jewelled crowns that kings have hurled
In shadowy pools, when armies fled;
The love-tales wrought with silken thread
By dreaming ladies upon cloth
That has made fat the murderous moth;
The roses that of old time were
Woven by ladies in their hair,
The dew-cold lilies ladies bore
Through many a sacred corridor
Where such grey clouds of incense rose
That only God's eyes did not close:

For that pale breast and lingering hand
Come from a more dream-heavy land,
A more dream-heavy hour than this;
And when you sigh from kiss to kiss
I hear white Beauty sighing, too,
For hours when all must fade like dew,
But flame on flame, and deep on deep,
Throne over throne where in half sleep,
Their swords upon their iron knees,
Brood her high lonely mysteries.

HE GIVES HIS BELOVED CERTAIN RHYMES

FASTEN your hair with a golden pin,
And bind up every wandering tress;
I bade my heart build these poor rhymes:
It worked at them, day out, day in,
Building a sorrowful loveliness
Out of the battles of old times.

You need but lift a pearl-pale hand,
And bind up your long hair and sigh;
And all men's hearts must burn and beat;
And candle-like foam on the dim sand,
And stars climbing the dew-dropping sky,
Live but to light your passing feet.

THE CAP AND BELLS

THE jester walked in the garden:
The garden had fallen still;
He bade his soul rise upward
And stand on her window-sill.

It rose in a straight blue garment,
When owls began to call:
It had grown wise-tongued by thinking
Of a quiet and light footfall;

But the young queen would not listen;
She rose in her pale night-gown;
She drew in the heavy casement
And pushed the latches down.

He bade his heart go to her,
When the owls called out no more;
In a red and quivering garment
It sang to her through the door.

It had grown sweet-tongued by dreaming
Of a flutter of flower-like hair;
But she took up her fan from the table
And waved it off on the air.

'I have cap and bells,' he pondered,
'I will send them to her and die';
And when the morning whitened
He left them where she went by.

She laid them upon her bosom,
Under a cloud of her hair,
And her red lips sang them a love-song
Till stars grew out of the air.

She opened her door and her window,
And the heart and the soul came through,
To her right hand came the red one,
To her left hand came the blue.

They set up a noise like crickets,
A chattering wise and sweet,
And her hair was a folded flower
And the quiet of love in her feet.

THE VALLEY OF THE BLACK PIG

THE dews drop slowly and dreams gather: unknown spears
Suddenly hurtle before my dream-awakened eyes,
And then the clash of fallen horsemen and the cries
Of unknown perishing armies beat about my ears.
We who still labour by the cromlech on the shore,
The grey cairn on the hill, when day sinks drowned in dew,
Being weary of the world's empires, bow down to you,
Master of the still stars and of the flaming door.

THE WIND AMONG THE REEDS

HE HEARS THE CRY OF THE SEDGE

I WANDER by the edge
Of this desolate lake
Where wind cries in the sedge:
Until the axle break
That keeps the stars in their round,
And hands hurl in the deep
The banners of East and West,
And the girdle of light is unbound,
Your breast will not lie by the breast
Of your beloved in sleep.

THE SECRET ROSE

FAR-OFF, most secret, and inviolate Rose,
Enfold me in my hour of hours; where those
Who sought thee in the Holy Sepulchre,
Or in the wine-vat, dwell beyond the stir
And tumult of defeated dreams; and deep
Among pale eyelids, heavy with the sleep
Men have named beauty. Thy great leaves enfold
The ancient beards, the helms of ruby and gold
Of the crowned Magi; and the king whose eyes
Saw the Pierced Hands and Rood of elder rise
In Druid vapour and make the torches dim;
Till vain frenzy awoke and he died; and him
Who met Fand walking among flaming dew
By a grey shore where the wind never blew,
And lost the world and Emer for a kiss;
And him who drove the gods out of their liss,

And till a hundred morns had flowered red
Feasted, and wept the barrows of his dead;
And the proud dreaming king who flung the crown
And sorrow away, and calling bard and clown
Dwelt among wine-stained wanderers in deep woods;
And him who sold tillage, and house, and goods,
And sought through lands and islands numberless years,
Until he found, with laughter and with tears,
A woman of so shining loveliness
That men threshed corn at midnight by a tress,
A little stolen tress. I, too, await
The hour of thy great wind of love and hate.
When shall the stars be blown about the sky,
Like the sparks blown out of a smithy, and die?
Surely thine hour has come, thy great wind blows,
Far-off, most secret, and inviolate Rose?

THE TRAVAIL OF PASSION

WHEN the flaming lute-thronged angelic door is wide;
When an immortal passion breathes in mortal clay;
Our hearts endure the scourge, the plaited thorns, the way
Crowded with bitter faces, the wounds in palm and side,
The vinegar-heavy sponge, the flowers by Kedron stream;
We will bend down and loosen our hair over you,
That it may drop faint perfume, and be heavy with dew,
Lilies of death-pale hope, roses of passionate dream.

HE WISHES HIS BELOVED WERE DEAD

WERE you but lying cold and dead,
And lights were paling out of the West,
You would come hither, and bend your head,
And I would lay my head on your breast;
And you would murmur tender words,
Forgiving me, because you were dead:
Nor would you rise and hasten away,
Though you have the will of the wild birds,
But know your hair was bound and wound
About the stars and moon and sun:
O would, beloved, that you lay
Under the dock-leaves in the ground,
While lights were paling one by one.

HE WISHES FOR THE CLOTHS OF HEAVEN

HAD I the heavens' embroidered cloths,
Enwrought with golden and silver light,
The blue and the dim and the dark cloths
Of night and light and the half-light,
I would spread the cloths under your feet:
But I, being poor, have only my dreams;
I have spread my dreams under your feet;
Tread softly because you tread on my dreams.

HE THINKS OF HIS PAST GREATNESS WHEN A PART OF THE CONSTELLATIONS OF HEAVEN

I HAVE drunk ale from the Country of the Young
And weep because I know all things now:
I have been a hazel-tree, and they hung
The Pilot Star and the Crooked Plough
Among my leaves in times out of mind:
I became a rush that horses tread:
I became a man, a hater of the wind,
Knowing one, out of all things, alone, that his head
May not lie on the breast nor his lips on the hair
Of the woman that he loves, until he dies.
O beast of the wilderness, bird of the air,
Must I endure your amorous cries?

THE FIDDLER OF DOONEY

WHEN I play on my fiddle in Dooney,
Folk dance like a wave of the sea;
My cousin is priest in Kilvarnet,
My brother in Mocharabuiee.[1]

I passed my brother and cousin:
They read in their books of prayer;
I read in my book of songs
I bought at the Sligo fair.

When we come at the end of time
To Peter sitting in state,
He will smile on the three old spirits,
But call me first through the gate;

[1] Pronounced as if spelt 'Mockrabwee'.

For the good are always the merry,
Save by an evil chance,
And the merry love the fiddle,
And the merry love to dance:

And when the folk there spy me,
They will all come up to me,
With 'Here is the fiddler of Dooney!'
And dance like a wave of the sea.

From *IN THE SEVEN WOODS*

THE ARROW

I THOUGHT of your beauty, and this arrow,
Made out of a wild thought, is in my marrow.
There's no man may look upon her, no man,
As when newly grown to be a woman,
Tall and noble but with face and bosom
Delicate in colour as apple blossom.
This beauty's kinder, yet for a reason
I could weep that the old is out of season.

NEVER GIVE ALL THE HEART

NEVER give all the heart, for love
Will hardly seem worth thinking of
To passionate women if it seem
Certain, and they never dream
That it fades out from kiss to kiss;
For everything that's lovely is
But a brief, dreamy, kind delight.
O never give the heart outright,
For they, for all smooth lips can say,
Have given their hearts up to the play.
And who could play it well enough
If deaf and dumb and blind with love?
He that made this knows all the cost,
For he gave all his heart and lost.

RED HANRAHAN'S SONG ABOUT IRELAND

THE old brown thorn-trees break in two high over Cummen
    Strand,
Under a bitter black wind that blows from the left hand;
Our courage breaks like an old tree in a black wind and dies,
But we have hidden in our hearts the flame out of the eyes
Of Cathleen, the daughter of Houlihan.

The wind has bundled up the clouds high over Knocknarea,
And thrown the thunder on the stones for all that Maeve can
    say.
Angers that are like noisy clouds have set our hearts abeat;
But we have all bent low and low and kissed the quiet feet
Of Cathleen, the daughter of Houlihan.

The yellow pool has overflowed high up on Clooth-na-Bare
For the wet winds are blowing out of the clinging air;
Like heavy flooded waters our bodies and our blood;
But purer than a tall candle before the Holy Rood
Is Cathleen, the daughter of Houlihan.

UNDER THE MOON

I HAVE no happiness in dreaming of Brycelinde,
Nor Avalon the grass-green hollow, nor Joyous Isle,
Where one found Lancelot crazed and hid him for a while;
Nor Uladh, when Naoise had thrown a sail upon the wind;
Nor lands that seem too dim to be burdens on the heart:
Land-under-Wave, where out of the moon's light and the
    sun's
Seven old sisters wind the threads of the long-lived ones,

Land-of-the-Tower, where Aengus has thrown the gates
    apart,
And Wood-of-Wonders, where one kills an ox at dawn,
To find it when night falls laid on a golden bier.
Therein are many queens like Branwen and Guinevere;
And Niamh and Laban and Fand, who could change to an
    otter or fawn,
And the wood-woman, whose lover was changed to a blue-
    eyed hawk;
And whether I go in my dreams by woodland, or dun, or
    shore,
Or on the unpeopled waves with kings to pull at the oar,
I hear the harp-string praise them, or hear their mournful
    talk.

Because of something told under the famished horn
Of the hunter's moon, that hung between the night and the
    day,
To dream of women whose beauty was folded in dismay,
Even in an old story, is a burden not to be borne.

O DO NOT LOVE TOO LONG

SWEETHEART, do not love too long:
I loved long and long,
And grew to be out of fashion
Like an old song.

All through the years of our youth
Neither could have known
Their own thought from the other's,
We were so much at one.

But O, in a minute she changed —
O do not love too long,
Or you will grow out of fashion
Like an old song.

THE HAPPY TOWNLAND

THERE'S many a strong farmer
Whose heart would break in two,
If he could see the townland
That we are riding to;
Boughs have their fruit and blossom
At all times of the year;
Rivers are running over
With red beer and brown beer.
An old man plays the bagpipes
In a golden and silver wood;
Queens, their eyes blue like the ice,
Are dancing in a crowd.

The little fox he murmured,
'O what of the world's bane?'
The sun was laughing sweetly,
The moon plucked at my rein;
But the little red fox murmured,
'O do not pluck at his rein,
He is riding to the townland
That is the world's bane.'

When their hearts are so high
That they would come to blows,
They unhook their heavy swords
From golden and silver boughs;
But all that are killed in battle
Awaken to life again.
It is lucky that their story
Is not known among men,
For O, the strong farmers
That would let the spade lie,
Their hearts would be like a cup
That somebody had drunk dry.

The little fox he murmured,
'O what of the world's bane?'
The sun was laughing sweetly,
The moon plucked at my rein;
But the little red fox murmured,
'O do not pluck at his rein,
He is riding to the townland
That is the world's bane.'

Michael will unhook his trumpet
From a bough overhead,
And blow a little noise
When the supper has been spread.
Gabriel will come from the water
With a fish-tail, and talk
Of wonders that have happened
On wet roads where men walk,
And lift up an old horn
Of hammered silver, and drink
Till he has fallen asleep
Upon the starry brink.

The little fox he murmured,
'O what of the world's bane?'
The sun was laughing sweetly,
The moon plucked at my rein;
But the little red fox murmured,
'O do not pluck at his rein,
He is riding to the townland
That is the world's bane.'

From *THE GREEN HELMET AND OTHER POEMS*

WORDS

I HAD this thought a while ago,
'My darling cannot understand
What I have done, or what would do
In this blind bitter land.'

And I grew weary of the sun
Until my thoughts cleared up again,
Remembering that the best I have done
Was done to make it plain;

That every year I have cried, 'At length
My darling understands it all,
Because I have come into my strength,
And words obey my call';

That had she done so who can say
What would have shaken from the sieve?
I might have thrown poor words away
And been content to live.

NO SECOND TROY

WHY should I blame her that she filled my days
With misery, or that she would of late
Have taught to ignorant men most violent ways,
Or hurled the little streets upon the great,

Had they but courage equal to desire?
What could have made her peaceful with a mind
That nobleness made simple as a fire,
With beauty like a tightened bow, a kind
That is not natural in an age like this,
Being high and solitary and most stern?
Why, what could she have done, being what she is?
Was there another Troy for her to burn?

RECONCILIATION

SOME may have blamed you that you took away
The verses that could move them on the day
When, the ears being deafened, the sight of the eyes blind
With lightning, you went from me, and I could find
Nothing to make a song about but kings,
Helmets, and swords, and half-forgotten things
That were like memories of you — but now
We'll out, for the world lives as long ago;
And while we're in our laughing, weeping fit,
Hurl helmets, crowns, and swords into the pit.
But, dear, cling close to me; since you were gone,
My barren thoughts have chilled me to the bone.

THE COMING OF WISDOM WITH TIME

THOUGH leaves are many, the root is one;
Through all the lying days of my youth
I swayed my leaves and flowers in the sun;
Now I may wither into the truth.

THE MASK

'Put off that mask of burning gold
With emerald eyes.'
'O no, my dear, you make so bold
To find if hearts be wild and wise,
And yet not cold.'

'I would but find what's there to find,
Love or deceit.'
'It was the mask engaged your mind,
And after set your heart to beat,
Not what's behind.'

'But lest you are my enemy,
I must enquire.'
'O no, my dear, let all that be;
What matter, so there is but fire
In you, in me?'

UPON A HOUSE SHAKEN BY THE LAND AGITATION

How should the world be luckier if this house,
Where passion and precision have been one
Time out of mind, became too ruinous
To breed the lidless eye that loves the sun?
And the sweet laughing eagle thoughts that grow
Where wings have memory of wings, and all
That comes of the best knit to the best? Although
Mean roof-trees were the sturdier for its fall,

How should their luck run high enough to reach
The gifts that govern men, and after these
To gradual Time's last gift, a written speech
Wrought of high laughter, loveliness and ease?

AT GALWAY RACES

There where the course is,
Delight makes all of the one mind,
The riders upon the galloping horses,
The crowd that closes in behind:
We, too, had good attendance once,
Hearers and hearteners of the work;
Aye, horsemen for companions,
Before the merchant and the clerk
Breathed on the world with timid breath.
Sing on: somewhere at some new moon,
We'll learn that sleeping is not death,
Hearing the whole earth change its tune,
Its flesh being wild, and it again
Crying aloud as the racecourse is,
And we find hearteners among men
That ride upon horses.

ALL THINGS CAN TEMPT ME

All things can tempt me from this craft of verse:
One time it was a woman's face, or worse —
The seeming needs of my fool-driven land;
Now nothing but comes readier to the hand

Than this accustomed toil. When I was young,
I had not given a penny for a song
Did not the poet sing it with such airs
That one believed he had a sword upstairs;
Yet would be now, could I but have my wish,
Colder and dumber and deafer than a fish.

From *RESPONSIBILITIES*

INTRODUCTORY RHYMES

*Pardon, old fathers, if you still remain
Somewhere in ear-shot for the story's end,
Old Dublin merchant 'free of the ten and four'
Or trading out of Galway into Spain;
Old country scholar, Robert Emmet's friend,
A hundred-year-old memory to the poor;
Merchant and scholar who have left me blood
That has not passed through any huckster's loin,
Soldiers that gave, whatever die was cast:
A Butler or an Armstrong that withstood
Beside the brackish waters of the Boyne
James and his Irish when the Dutchman crossed;
Old merchant skipper that leaped overboard
After a ragged hat in Biscay Bay;
You most of all, silent and fierce old man,
Because the daily spectacle that stirred
My fancy, and set my boyish lips to say,
'Only the wasteful virtues earn the sun';
Pardon that for a barren passion's sake,
Although I have come close on forty-nine,
I have no child, I have nothing but a book,
Nothing but that to prove your blood and mine.*

January 1914

THE GREY ROCK

POETS with whom I learned my trade,
Companions of the Cheshire Cheese,
Here's an old story I've remade,
Imagining 'twould better please
Your ears than stories now in fashion,
Though you may think I waste my breath
Pretending that there can be passion
That has more life in it than death,
And though at bottling of your wine
Old wholesome Goban had no say;
The moral's yours because it's mine.

When cups went round at close of day —
Is not that how good stories run? —
The gods were sitting at the board
In their great house at Slievenamon.
They sang a drowsy song, or snored,
For all were full of wine and meat.
The smoky torches made a glare
On metal Goban 'd hammered at,
On old deep silver rolling there
Or on some still unemptied cup
That he, when frenzy stirred his thews,
Had hammered out on mountain top
To hold the sacred stuff he brews
That only gods may buy of him.
Now from that juice that made them wise
All those had lifted up the dim
Imaginations of their eyes,
For one that was like woman made

Before their sleepy eyelids ran
And trembling with her passion said,
'Come out and dig for a dead man,
Who's burrowing somewhere in the ground,
And mock him to his face and then
Hollo him on with horse and hound,
For he is the worst of all dead men.'

We should be dazed and terror-struck,
If we but saw in dreams that room,
Those wine-drenched eyes, and curse our luck
That emptied all our days to come.
I knew a woman none could please,
Because she dreamed when but a child
Of men and women made like these;
And after, when her blood ran wild,
Had ravelled her own story out,
And said, 'In two or in three years
I needs must marry some poor lout,'
And having said it, burst in tears.

Since, tavern comrades, you have died,
Maybe your images have stood,
Mere bone and muscle thrown aside,
Before that roomful or as good.
You had to face your ends when young —
'Twas wine or women, or some curse —
But never made a poorer song
That you might have a heavier purse,
Nor gave loud service to a cause
That you might have a troop of friends.
You kept the Muses' sterner laws,
And unrepenting faced your ends,

And therefore earned the right — and yet
Dowson and Johnson most I praise —
To troop with those the world's forgot,
And copy their proud steady gaze.

'The Danish troop was driven out
Between the dawn and dusk,' she said;
'Although the event was long in doubt,
Although the King of Ireland's dead
And half the kings, before sundown
All was accomplished.
               'When this day
Murrough, the King of Ireland's son,
Foot after foot was giving way,
He and his best troops back to back
Had perished there, but the Danes ran,
Stricken with panic from the attack,
The shouting of an unseen man;
And being thankful Murrough found,
Led by a footsole dipped in blood
That had made prints upon the ground,
Where by old thorn-trees that man stood;
And though when he gazed here and there,
He had but gazed on thorn-trees, spoke,
"Who is the friend that seems but air
And yet could give so fine a stroke?"
Thereon a young man met his eye,
Who said, "Because she held me in
Her love, and would not have me die,
Rock-nurtured Aoife took a pin,
And pushing it into my shirt,
Promised that for a pin's sake
No man should see to do me hurt:

But there it's gone; I will not take
The fortune that had been my shame
Seeing, King's son, what wounds you have."
'Twas roundly spoke, but when night came
He had betrayed me to his grave,
For he and the King's son were dead.
I'd promised him two hundred years,
And when for all I'd done or said —
And these immortal eyes shed tears —
He claimed his country's need was most,
I'd saved his life, yet for the sake
Of a new friend he has turned a ghost.
What does he care if my heart break?
I call for spade and horse and hound
That we may harry him.' Thereon
She cast herself upon the ground
And rent her clothes and made her moan:
'Why are they faithless when their might
Is from the holy shades that rove
The grey rock and the windy light?
Why should the faithfullest heart most love
The bitter sweetness of false faces?
Why must the lasting love what passes,
Why are the gods by men betrayed?'

But thereon every god stood up
With a slow smile and without sound,
And stretching forth his arm and cup
To where she moaned upon the ground,
Suddenly drenched her to the skin;
And she with Goban's wine adrip,
No more remembering what had been,
Stared at the gods with laughing lip.

I have kept my faith, though faith was tried,
To that rock-born, rock-wandering foot,
And the world's altered since you died,
And I am in no good repute
With the loud host before the sea,
That think sword-strokes were better meant
Than lover's music — let that be,
So that the wandering foot's content.

TO A WEALTHY MAN WHO PROMISED A SECOND SUBSCRIPTION TO THE DUBLIN MUNICIPAL GALLERY IF IT WERE PROVED THE PEOPLE WANTED PICTURES

You gave, but will not give again
Until enough of Paudeen's pence
By Biddy's halfpennies have lain
To be 'some sort of evidence',
Before you'll put your guineas down,
That things it were a pride to give
Are what the blind and ignorant town
Imagines best to make it thrive.
What cared Duke Ercole, that bid
His mummers to the market-place,
What th' onion-sellers thought or did
So that his Plautus set the pace
For the Italian comedies?
And Guidobaldo, when he made
That grammar school of courtesies
Where wit and beauty learned their trade

Upon Urbino's windy hill,
Had sent no runners to and fro
That he might learn the shepherds' will.
And when they drove out Cosimo,
Indifferent how the rancour ran,
He gave the hours they had set free
To Michelozzo's latest plan
For the San Marco Library,
Whence turbulent Italy should draw
Delight in Art whose end is peace,
In logic and in natural law
By sucking at the dugs of Greece.

Your open hand but shows our loss,
For he knew better how to live.
Let Paudeens play at pitch and toss,
Look up in the sun's eye and give
What the exultant heart calls good
That some new day may breed the best
Because you gave, not what they would,
But the right twigs for an eagle's nest!

December 1912

SEPTEMBER 1913

WHAT need you, being come to sense,
But fumble in a greasy till
And add the halfpence to the pence
And prayer to shivering prayer, until
You have dried the marrow from the bone?
For men were born to pray and save:
Romantic Ireland's dead and gone,
It's with O'Leary in the grave.

Yet they were of a different kind,
The names that stilled your childish play,
They have gone about the world like wind,
But little time had they to pray
For whom the hangman's rope was spun,
And what, God help us, could they save?
Romantic Ireland's dead and gone,
It's with O'Leary in the grave.

Was it for this the wild geese spread
The grey wing upon every tide;
For this that all that blood was shed,
For this Edward Fitzgerald died,
And Robert Emmet and Wolfe Tone,
All that delirium of the brave?
Romantic Ireland's dead and gone,
It's with O'Leary in the grave.

Yet could we turn the years again,
And call those exiles as they were
In all their loneliness and pain,
You'd cry, 'Some woman's yellow hair
Has maddened every mother's son':
They weighed so lightly what they gave.
But let them be, they're dead and gone,
They're with O'Leary in the grave.

TO A SHADE

IF you have revisited the town, thin Shade,
Whether to look upon your monument
(I wonder if the builder has been paid)
Or happier-thoughted when the day is spent
To drink of that salt breath out of the sea
When grey gulls flit about instead of men,
And the gaunt houses put on majesty:
Let these content you and be gone again;
For they are at their old tricks yet.

                                  A man
Of your own passionate serving kind who had brought
In his full hands what, had they only known,
Had given their children's children loftier thought,
Sweeter emotion, working in their veins
Like gentle blood, has been driven from the place,
And insult heaped upon him for his pains,
And for his open-handedness, disgrace;
Your enemy, an old foul mouth, had set
The pack upon him.

                        Go, unquiet wanderer,
And gather the Glasnevin coverlet
About your head till the dust stops your ear,
The time for you to taste of that salt breath
And listen at the corners has not come:
You had enough of sorrow before death —
Away, away! You are safer in the tomb.

September 29, 1913

THE THREE HERMITS

THREE old hermits took the air
By a cold and desolate sea,
First was muttering a prayer,
Second rummaged for a flea;
On a windy stone, the third,
Giddy with his hundredth year,
Sang unnoticed like a bird:
'Though the Door of Death is near
And what waits behind the door,
Three times in a single day
I, though upright on the shore,
Fall asleep when I should pray.'
So the first, but now the second:
'We're but given what we have earned
When all thoughts and deeds are reckoned,
So it's plain to be discerned
That the shades of holy men
Who have failed, being weak of will,
Pass the Door of Birth again,
And are plagued by crowds, until
They've the passion to escape.'
Moaned the other, 'They are thrown
Into some most fearful shape.'
But the second mocked his moan:
'They are not changed to anything,
Having loved God once, but maybe
To a poet or a king
Or a witty lovely lady.'
While he'd rummaged rags and hair,

Caught and cracked his flea, the third,
Giddy with his hundredth year,
Sang unnoticed like a bird.

BEGGAR TO BEGGAR CRIED

'TIME to put off the world and go somewhere
And find my health again in the sea air,'
Beggar to beggar cried, being frenzy-struck,
'And make my soul before my pate is bare.'

'And get a comfortable wife and house
To rid me of the devil in my shoes,'
Beggar to beggar cried, being frenzy-struck,
'And the worse devil that is between my thighs.'

'And though I'd marry with a comely lass,
She need not be too comely — let it pass,'
Beggar to beggar cried, being frenzy-struck,
'But there's a devil in a looking-glass.'

'Nor should she be too rich, because the rich
Are driven by wealth as beggars by the itch,'
Beggar to beggar cried, being frenzy-struck,
'And cannot have a humorous happy speech.'

'And there I'll grow respected at my ease,
And hear amid the garden's nightly peace,'
Beggar to beggar cried, being frenzy-struck,
'The wind-blown clamour of the barnacle-geese.'

THE MOUNTAIN TOMB

POUR wine and dance if manhood still have pride,
Bring roses if the rose be yet in bloom;
The cataract smokes upon the mountain side,
Our Father Rosicross is in his tomb.

Pull down the blinds, bring fiddle and clarionet
That there be no foot silent in the room
Nor mouth from kissing, nor from wine unwet;
Our Father Rosicross is in his tomb.

In vain, in vain; the cataract still cries;
The everlasting taper lights the gloom;
All wisdom shut into his onyx eyes,
Our Father Rosicross sleeps in his tomb.

TO A CHILD DANCING IN THE WIND

DANCE there upon the shore;
What need have you to care
For wind or water's roar?
And tumble out your hair
That the salt drops have wet;
Being young you have not known
The fool's triumph, nor yet
Love lost as soon as won,
Nor the best labourer dead
And all the sheaves to bind.
What need have you to dread
The monstrous crying of wind?

FRIENDS

Now must I these three praise —
Three women that have wrought
What joy is in my days:
One because no thought,
Nor those unpassing cares,
No, not in these fifteen
Many-times-troubled years,
Could ever come between
Mind and delighted mind;
And one because her hand
Had strength that could unbind
What none can understand,
What none can have and thrive,
Youth's dreamy load, till she
So changed me that I live
Labouring in ecstasy.
And what of her that took
All till my youth was gone
With scarce a pitying look?
How could I praise that one?
When day begins to break
I count my good and bad,
Being wakeful for her sake,
Remembering what she had,
What eagle look still shows,
While up from my heart's root
So great a sweetness flows
I shake from head to foot.

THE COLD HEAVEN

SUDDENLY I saw the cold and rook-delighting heaven
That seemed as though ice burned and was but the more ice,
And thereupon imagination and heart were driven
So wild that every casual thought of that and this
Vanished, and left but memories, that should be out of
      season
With the hot blood of youth, of love crossed long ago;
And I took all the blame out of all sense and reason,
Until I cried and trembled and rocked to and fro,
Riddled with light. Ah! when the ghost begins to quicken,
Confusion of the death-bed over, is it sent
Out naked on the roads, as the books say, and stricken
By the injustice of the skies for punishment?

AN APPOINTMENT

BEING out of heart with government
I took a broken root to fling
Where the proud, wayward squirrel went,
Taking delight that he could spring;
And he, with that low whinnying sound
That is like laughter, sprang again
And so to the other tree at a bound.
Nor the tame will, nor timid brain,
Nor heavy knitting of the brow
Bred that fierce tooth and cleanly limb
And threw him up to laugh on the bough;
No government appointed him.

THE MAGI

Now as at all times I can see in the mind's eye,
In their stiff, painted clothes, the pale unsatisfied ones
Appear and disappear in the blue depth of the sky
With all their ancient faces like rain-beaten stones,
And all their helms of silver hovering side by side,
And all their eyes still fixed, hoping to find once more,
Being by Calvary's turbulence unsatisfied,
The uncontrollable mystery on the bestial floor.

A COAT

I MADE my song a coat
Covered with embroideries
Out of old mythologies
From heel to throat;
But the fools caught it,
Wore it in the world's eyes
As though they'd wrought it.
Song, let them take it,
For there's more enterprise
In walking naked.

From *THE WILD SWANS AT COOLE*

THE WILD SWANS AT COOLE

THE trees are in their autumn beauty,
The woodland paths are dry,
Under the October twilight the water
Mirrors a still sky;
Upon the brimming water among the stones
Are nine-and-fifty swans.

The nineteenth autumn has come upon me
Since I first made my count;
I saw, before I had well finished,
All suddenly mount
And scatter wheeling in great broken rings
Upon their clamorous wings.

I have looked upon those brilliant creatures,
And now my heart is sore.
All's changed since I, hearing at twilight,
The first time on this shore,
The bell-beat of their wings above my head,
Trod with a lighter tread.

Unwearied still, lover by lover,
They paddle in the cold
Companionable streams or climb the air;
Their hearts have not grown old;
Passion or conquest, wander where they will,
Attend upon them still.

But now they drift on the still water,
Mysterious, beautiful;
Among what rushes will they build,
By what lake's edge or pool
Delight men's eyes when I awake some day
To find they have flown away?

IN MEMORY OF MAJOR ROBERT GREGORY

I

Now that we're almost settled in our house
I'll name the friends that cannot sup with us
Beside a fire of turf in th' ancient tower,
And having talked to some late hour
Climb up the narrow winding stair to bed:
Discoverers of forgotten truth
Or mere companions of my youth,
All, all are in my thoughts to-night being dead.

II

Always we'd have the new friend meet the old
And we are hurt if either friend seem cold,
And there is salt to lengthen out the smart
In the affections of our heart,
And quarrels are blown up upon that head;
But not a friend that I would bring
This night can set us quarrelling,
For all that come into my mind are dead.

III

Lionel Johnson comes the first to mind,
That loved his learning better than mankind,

Though courteous to the worst; much falling he
Brooded upon sanctity
Till all his Greek and Latin learning seemed
A long blast upon the horn that brought
A little nearer to his thought
A measureless consummation that he dreamed.

IV

And that enquiring man John Synge comes next,
That dying chose the living world for text
And never could have rested in the tomb
But that, long travelling, he had come
Towards nightfall upon certain set apart
In a most desolate stony place,
Towards nightfall upon a race
Passionate and simple like his heart.

V

And then I think of old George Pollexfen,
In muscular youth well known to Mayo men
For horsemanship at meets or at racecourses,
That could have shown how pure-bred horses
And solid men, for all their passion, live
But as the outrageous stars incline
By opposition, square and trine;
Having grown sluggish and contemplative.

VI

They were my close companions many a year,
A portion of my mind and life, as it were,
And now their breathless faces seem to look
Out of some old picture-book;

I am accustomed to their lack of breath,
But not that my dear friend's dear son,
Our Sidney and our perfect man,
Could share in that discourtesy of death.

VII

For all things the delighted eye now sees
Were loved by him: the old storm-broken trees
That cast their shadows upon road and bridge;
The tower set on the stream's edge;
The ford where drinking cattle make a stir
Nightly, and startled by that sound
The water-hen must change her ground;
He might have been your heartiest welcomer.

VIII

When with the galway foxhounds he would ride
From Castle Taylor to the Roxborough side
Or Esserkelly plain, few kept his pace;
At Mooneen he had leaped a place
So perilous that half the astonished meet
Had shut their eyes; and where was it
He rode a race without a bit?
And yet his mind outran the horses' feet.

IX

We dreamed that a great painter had been born
To cold Clare rock and Galway rock and thorn,
To that stern colour and that delicate line
That are our secret discipline
Wherein the gazing heart doubles her might.

Soldier, scholar, horseman, he,
And yet he had the intensity
To have published all to be a world's delight.

X

What other could so well have counselled us
In all lovely intricacies of a house
As he that practised or that understood
All work in metal or in wood,
In moulded plaster or in carven stone?
Soldier, scholar, horseman, he,
And all he did done perfectly
As though he had but that one trade alone.

XI

Some burn damp faggots, others may consume
The entire combustible world in one small room
As though dried straw, and if we turn about
The bare chimney is gone black out
Because the work had finished in that flare.
Soldier, scholar, horseman, he,
As 'twere all life's epitome.
What made us dream that he could comb grey hair?

XII

I had thought, seeing how bitter is that wind
That shakes the shutter, to have brought to mind
All those that manhood tried, or childhood loved
Or boyish intellect approved,
With some appropriate commentary on each;
Until imagination brought
A fitter welcome; but a thought
Of that late death took all my heart for speech.

AN IRISH AIRMAN FORESEES HIS DEATH

I KNOW that I shall meet my fate
Somewhere among the clouds above;
Those that I fight I do not hate,
Those that I guard I do not love;
My country is Kiltartan Cross,
My countrymen Kiltartan's poor,
No likely end could bring them loss
Or leave them happier than before.
Nor law, nor duty bade me fight,
Nor public men, nor cheering crowds,
A lonely impulse of delight
Drove to this tumult in the clouds;
I balanced all, brought all to mind,
The years to come seemed waste of breath,
A waste of breath the years behind
In balance with this life, this death.

TO A YOUNG BEAUTY

DEAR fellow-artist, why so free
With every sort of company,
With every Jack and Jill?
Choose your companions from the best;
Who draws a bucket with the rest
Soon topples down the hill.

You may, that mirror for a school,
Be passionate, not bountiful
As common beauties may,

Who were not born to keep in trim
With old Ezekiel's cherubim
But those of Beauvarlet.

I know what wages beauty gives,
How hard a life her servant lives,
Yet praise the winters gone:
There is not a fool can call me friend,
And I may dine at journey's end
With Landor and with Donne.

TO A YOUNG GIRL

My dear, my dear, I know
More than another
What makes your heart beat so;
Not even your own mother
Can know it as I know,
Who broke my heart for her
When the wild thought,
That she denies
And has forgot,
Set all her blood astir
And glittered in her eyes.

THE SCHOLARS

BALD heads forgetful of their sins,
Old learned, respectable bald heads
Edit and annotate the lines
That young men, tossing on their beds,
Rhymed out in love's despair
To flatter beauty's ignorant ear.

All shuffle there; all cough in ink;
All wear the carpet with their shoes;
All think what other people think;
All know the man their neighbour knows.
Lord, what would they say
Did their Catullus walk that way?

THE FISHERMAN

ALTHOUGH I can see him still,
The freckled man who goes
To a grey place on a hill
In grey Connemara clothes
At dawn to cast his flies,
It's long since I began
To call up to the eyes
This wise and simple man.
All day I'd looked in the face
What I had hoped 'twould be
To write for my own race
And the reality;

The living men that I hate,
The dead man that I loved,
The craven man in his seat,
The insolent unreproved,
And no knave brought to book
Who has won a drunken cheer,
The witty man and his joke
Aimed at the commonest ear,
The clever man who cries
The catch-cries of the clown,
The beating down of the wise
And great Art beaten down.

Maybe a twelvemonth since
Suddenly I began,
In scorn of this audience,
Imagining a man,
And his sun-freckled face,
And grey Connemara cloth,
Climbing up to a place
Where stone is dark under froth,
And the down-turn of his wrist
When the flies drop in the stream;
A man who does not exist,
A man who is but a dream;
And cried, 'Before I am old
I shall have written him one
Poem maybe as cold
And passionate as the dawn.'

HER PRAISE

She is foremost of those that I would hear praised.
I have gone about the house, gone up and down
As a man does who has published a new book,
Or a young girl dressed out in her new gown,
And though I have turned the talk by hook or crook
Until her praise should be the uppermost theme,
A woman spoke of some new tale she had read,
A man confusedly in a half dream
As though some other name ran in his head.
She is foremost of those that I would hear praised.
I will talk no more of books or the long war
But walk by the dry thorn until I have found
Some beggar sheltering from the wind, and there
Manage the talk until her name come round.
If there be rags enough he will know her name
And be well pleased remembering it, for in the old days,
Though she had young men's praise and old men's blame,
Among the poor both old and young gave her praise.

THE PEOPLE

'What have I earned for all that work,' I said,
'For all that I have done at my own charge?
The daily spite of this unmannerly town,
Where who has served the most is most defamed,
The reputation of his lifetime lost
Between the night and morning. I might have lived,
And you know well how great the longing has been,

Where every day my footfall should have lit
In the green shadow of Ferrara wall;
Or climbed among the images of the past —
The unperturbed and courtly images —
Evening and morning, the steep street of Urbino
To where the Duchess and her people talked
The stately midnight through until they stood
In their great window looking at the dawn;
I might have had no friend that could not mix
Courtesy and passion into one like those
That saw the wicks grow yellow in the dawn;
I might have used the one substantial right
My trade allows: chosen my company,
And chosen what scenery had pleased me best.'
Thereon my phoenix answered in reproof,
'The drunkards, pilferers of public funds,
All the dishonest crowd I had driven away,
When my luck changed and they dared meet my face,
Crawled from obscurity, and set upon me
Those I had served and some that I had fed;
Yet never have I, now nor any time,
Complained of the people.'

                           All I could reply
Was: 'You, that have not lived in thought but deed,
Can have the purity of a natural force,
But I, whose virtues are the definitions
Of the analytic mind, can neither close
The eye of the mind nor keep my tongue from speech.'
And yet, because my heart leaped at her words,
I was abashed, and now they come to mind
After nine years, I sink my head abashed.

BROKEN DREAMS

THERE is grey in your hair.
Young men no longer suddenly catch their breath
When you are passing;
But maybe some old gaffer mutters a blessing
Because it was your prayer
Recovered him upon the bed of death.
For your sole sake — that all heart's ache have known,
And given to others all heart's ache,
From meagre girlhood's putting on
Burdensome beauty — for your sole sake
Heaven has put away the stroke of her doom,
So great her portion in that peace you make
By merely walking in a room.

Your beauty can but leave among us
Vague memories, nothing but memories.
A young man when the old men are done talking
Will say to an old man, 'Tell me of that lady
The poet stubborn with his passion sang us
When age might well have chilled his blood.'

Vague memories, nothing but memories,
But in the grave all, all, shall be renewed.
The certainty that I shall see that lady
Leaning or standing or walking
In the first loveliness of womanhood,
And with the fervour of my youthful eyes,
Has set me muttering like a fool.

You are more beautiful than any one,
And yet your body had a flaw:

Your small hands were not beautiful,
And I am afraid that you will run
And paddle to the wrist
In that mysterious, always brimming lake
Where those that have obeyed the holy law
Paddle and are perfect. Leave unchanged
The hands that I have kissed,
For old sake's sake.

The last stroke of midnight dies.
All day in the one chair
From dream to dream and rhyme to rhyme I have ranged
In rambling talk with an image of air:
Vague memories, nothing but memories.

PRESENCES

THIS night has been so strange that it seemed
As if the hair stood up on my head.
From going-down of the sun I have dreamed
That women laughing, or timid or wild,
In rustle of lace or silken stuff,
Climbed up my creaking stair. They had read
All I had rhymed of that monstrous thing
Returned and yet unrequited love.
They stood in the door and stood between
My great wood lectern and the fire
Till I could hear their hearts beating:
One is a harlot, and one a child
That never looked upon man with desire,
And one, it may be, a queen.

EGO DOMINUS TUUS

Hic. On the grey sand beside the shallow stream
 Under your old wind-beaten tower, where still
 A lamp burns on beside the open book
 That Michael Robartes left, you walk in the moon,
 And, though you have passed the best of life, still trace,
 Enthralled by the unconquerable delusion,
 Magical shapes.

Ille.   By the help of an image
 I call to my own opposite, summon all
 That I have handled least, least looked upon.

Hic. And I would find myself and not an image.

Ille. That is our modern hope, and by its light
 We have lit upon the gentle, sensitive mind
 And lost the old nonchalance of the hand;
 Whether we have chosen chisel, pen or brush,
 We are but critics, or but half create,
 Timid, entangled, empty and abashed,
 Lacking the countenance of our friends.

Hic.   And yet
 The chief imagination of Christendom,
 Dante Alighieri, so utterly found himself
 That he has made that hollow face of his
 More plain to the mind's eye than any face
 But that of Christ.

Ille.   And did he find himself
  Or was the hunger that had made it hollow
  A hunger for the apple on the bough
  Most out of reach? and is that spectral image
  The man that Lapo and that Guido knew?
  I think he fashioned from his opposite
  An image that might have been a stony face
  Staring upon a Bedouin's horse-hair roof
  From doored and windowed cliff, or half upturned
  Among the coarse grass and the camel-dung.
  He set his chisel to the hardest stone.
  Being mocked by Guido for his lecherous life,
  Derided and deriding, driven out
  To climb that stair and eat that bitter bread,
  He found the unpersuadable justice, he found
  The most exalted lady loved by a man.

Hic. Yet surely there are men who have made their art
  Out of no tragic war, lovers of life,
  Impulsive men that look for happiness
  And sing when they have found it.

Ille.   No, not sing,
  For those that love the world serve it in action,
  Grow rich, popular and full of influence,
  And should they paint or write, still it is action:
  The struggle of the fly in marmalade.
  The rhetorician would deceive his neighbours,
  The sentimentalist himself; while art
  Is but a vision of reality.
  What portion in the world can the artist have
  Who has awakened from the common dream
  But dissipation and despair?

Hic.   And yet
   No one denies to Keats love of the world;
   Remember his deliberate happiness.

Ille. His art is happy, but who knows his mind?
   I see a schoolboy when I think of him,
   With face and nose pressed to a sweet-shop window,
   For certainly he sank into his grave
   His senses and his heart unsatisfied,
   And made — being poor, ailing and ignorant,
   Shut out from all the luxury of the world,
   The coarse-bred son of a livery-stable keeper —
   Luxuriant song.

Hic.   Why should you leave the lamp
   Burning alone beside an open book,
   And trace these characters upon the sands?
   A style is found by sedentary toil
   And by the imitation of great masters.

Ille. Because I seek an image, not a book.
   Those men that in their writings are most wise
   Own nothing but their blind, stupefied hearts.
   I call to the mysterious one who yet
   Shall walk the wet sands by the edge of the stream
   And look most like me, being indeed my double,
   And prove of all imaginable things
   The most unlike, being my anti-self,
   And, standing by these characters, disclose
   All that I seek; and whisper it as though
   He were afraid the birds, who cry aloud
   Their momentary cries before it is dawn,
   Would carry it away to blasphemous men.

THE PHASES OF THE MOON

AN old man cocked his ear upon a bridge;
He and his friend, their faces to the South,
Had trod the uneven road. Their boots were soiled,
Their Connemara cloth worn out of shape;
They had kept a steady pace as though their beds,
Despite a dwindling and late-risen moon,
Were distant still. An old man cocked his ear.

Aherne. What made that sound?

Robartes.   A rat or water-hen
  Splashed, or an otter slid into the stream.
  We are on the bridge; that shadow is the tower,
  And the light proves that he is reading still.
  He has found, after the manner of his kind,
  Mere images; chosen this place to live in
  Because, it may be, of the candle-light
  From the far tower where Milton's Platonist
  Sat late, or Shelley's visionary prince:
  The lonely light that Samuel Palmer engraved,
  An image of mysterious wisdom won by toil;
  And now he seeks in book or manuscript
  What he shall never find.

Aherne.   Why should not you
  Who know it all ring at his door, and speak
  Just truth enough to show that his whole life
  Will scarcely find for him a broken crust
  Of all those truths that are your daily bread;
  And when you have spoken take the roads again?

Robartes. He wrote of me in that extravagant style
He had learnt from Pater, and to round his tale
Said I was dead; and dead I choose to be.

Aherne. Sing me the changes of the moon once more;
True song, though speech: 'mine author sung it me.'

Robartes. Twenty-and-eight the phases of the moon,
The full and the moon's dark and all the crescents,
Twenty-and-eight, and yet but six-and-twenty
The cradles that a man must needs be rocked in:
For there's no human life at the full or the dark.
From the first crescent to the half, the dream
But summons to adventure and the man
Is always happy like a bird or a beast;
But while the moon is rounding towards the full
He follows whatever whim's most difficult
Among whims not impossible, and though scarred,
As with the cat-o'-nine-tails of the mind,
His body moulded from within his body
Grows comelier. Eleven pass, and then
Athene takes Achilles by the hair,
Hector is in the dust, Nietzsche is born,
Because the hero's crescent is the twelfth.
And yet, twice born, twice buried, grow he must,
Before the full moon, helpless as a worm.
The thirteenth moon but sets the soul at war
In its own being, and when that war's begun
There is no muscle in the arm; and after,
Under the frenzy of the fourteenth moon,
The soul begins to tremble into stillness,
To die into the labyrinth of itself!

Aherne. Sing out the song; sing to the end, and sing
   The strange reward of all that discipline.

Robartes. All thought becomes an image and the soul
   Becomes a body: that body and that soul
   Too perfect at the full to lie in a cradle,
   Too lonely for the traffic of the world:
   Body and soul cast out and cast away
   Beyond the visible world.

Aherne.   All dreams of the soul
   End in a beautiful man's or woman's body.

Robartes. Have you not always known it?

Aherne.   The song will have it
   That those that we have loved got their long fingers
   From death, and wounds, or on Sinai's top,
   Or from some bloody whip in their own hands.
   They ran from cradle to cradle till at last
   Their beauty dropped out of the loneliness
   Of body and soul.

Robartes.   The lover's heart knows that.

Aherne. It must be that the terror in their eyes
   Is memory or foreknowledge of the hour
   When all is fed with light and heaven is bare.

Robartes. When the moon's full those creatures of the full
   Are met on the waste hills by countrymen
   Who shudder and hurry by: body and soul
   Estranged amid the strangeness of themselves,
   Caught up in contemplation, the mind's eye
   Fixed upon images that once were thought;

For separate, perfect, and immovable
Images can break the solitude
Of lovely, satisfied, indifferent eyes.

And thereupon with aged, high-pitched voice
Aherne laughed, thinking of the man within,
His sleepless candle and laborious pen.

Robartes. And after that the crumbling of the moon.
The soul remembering its loneliness
Shudders in many cradles; all is changed,
It would be the world's servant, and as it serves,
Choosing whatever task's most difficult
Among tasks not impossible, it takes
Upon the body and upon the soul
The coarseness of the drudge.

Aherne.   Before the full
It sought itself and afterwards the world.

Robartes. Because you are forgotten, half out of life,
And never wrote a book, your thought is clear.
Reformer, merchant, statesman, learned man,
Dutiful husband, honest wife by turn,
Cradle upon cradle, and all in flight and all
Deformed because there is no deformity
But saves us from a dream.

Aherne.   And what of those
That the last servile crescent has set free?

Robartes. Because all dark, like those that are all light,
They are cast beyond the verge, and in a cloud,
Crying to one another like the bats;

And having no desire they cannot tell
What's good or bad, or what it is to triumph
At the perfection of one's own obedience;
And yet they speak what's blown into the mind;
Deformed beyond deformity, unformed,
Insipid as the dough before it is baked,
They change their bodies at a word.

Aherne.   And then?

Robartes. When all the dough has been so kneaded up
    That it can take what form cook Nature fancies,
    The first thin crescent is wheeled round once more.

Aherne. But the escape; the song's not finished yet.

Robartes. Hunchback and Saint and Fool are the last crescents.
    The burning bow that once could shoot an arrow
    Out of the up and down, the wagon-wheel
    Of beauty's cruelty and wisdom's chatter —
    Out of that raving tide — is drawn betwixt
    Deformity of body and of mind.

Aherne. Were not our beds far off I'd ring the bell,
    Stand under the rough roof-timbers of the hall
    Beside the castle door, where all is stark
    Austerity, a place set out for wisdom
    That he will never find; I'd play a part;
    He would never know me after all these years
    But take me for some drunken countryman;
    I'd stand and mutter there until he caught
    'Hunchback and Saint and Fool,' and that they came
    Under the three last crescents of the moon,
    And then I'd stagger out. He'd crack his wits
    Day after day, yet never find the meaning.

And then he laughed to think that what seemed hard
Should be so simple — a bat rose from the hazels
And circled round him with its squeaky cry,
The light in the tower window was put out.

THE CAT AND THE MOON

THE cat went here and there
And the moon spun round like a top,
And the nearest kin of the moon,
The creeping cat, looked up.
Black Minnaloushe stared at the moon,
For, wander and wail as he would,
The pure cold light in the sky
Troubled his animal blood.
Minnaloushe runs in the grass
Lifting his delicate feet.
Do you dance, Minnaloushe, do you dance?
When two close kindred meet,
What better than call a dance?
Maybe the moon may learn,
Tired of that courtly fashion,
A new dance turn.
Minnaloushe creeps through the grass
From moonlit place to place,
The sacred moon overhead
Has taken a new phase.
Does Minnaloushe know that his pupils
Will pass from change to change,
And that from round to crescent,
From crescent to round they range?

Minnaloushe creeps through the grass
Alone, important and wise,
And lifts to the changing moon
His changing eyes.

THE DOUBLE VISION OF MICHAEL ROBARTES

I

ON the grey rock of Cashel the mind's eye
Has called up the cold spirits that are born
When the old moon is vanished from the sky
And the new still hides her horn.

Under blank eyes and fingers never still
The particular is pounded till it is man.
When had I my own will?
O not since life began.

Constrained, arraigned, baffled, bent and unbent
By these wire-jointed jaws and limbs of wood,
Themselves obedient,
Knowing not evil and good;

Obedient to some hidden magical breath.
They do not even feel, so abstract are they,
So dead beyond our death,
Triumph that we obey.

II

On the grey rock of Cashel I suddenly saw
A Sphinx with woman breast and lion paw,
A Buddha, hand at rest,
Hand lifted up that blest;

And right between these two a girl at play
That, it may be, had danced her life away,
For now being dead it seemed
That she of dancing dreamed.

Although I saw it all in the mind's eye
There can be nothing solider till I die;
I saw by the moon's light
Now at its fifteenth night.

One lashed her tail; her eyes lit by the moon
Gazed upon all things known, all things unknown,
In triumph of intellect
With motionless head erect.

That other's moonlit eyeballs never moved,
Being fixed on all things loved, all things unloved,
Yet little peace he had,
For those that love are sad.

O little did they care who danced between,
And little she by whom her dance was seen
So she had outdanced thought.
Body perfection brought,

For what but eye and ear silence the mind
With the minute particulars of mankind?
Mind moved yet seemed to stop
As 'twere a spinning-top.

In contemplation had those three so wrought
Upon a moment, and so stretched it out
That they, time overthrown,
Were dead yet flesh and bone.

III

I knew that I had seen, had seen at last
That girl my unremembering nights hold fast
Or else my dreams that fly
If I should rub an eye,

And yet in flying fling into my meat
A crazy juice that makes the pulses beat
As though I had been undone
By Homer's Paragon

Who never gave the burning town a thought;
To such a pitch of folly I am brought,
Being caught between the pull
Of the dark moon and the full,

The commonness of thought and images
That have the frenzy of our western seas.
Thereon I made my moan,
And after kissed a stone,

And after that arranged it in a song
Seeing that I, ignorant for so long,
Had been rewarded thus
In Cormac's ruined house.

From *MICHAEL ROBARTES AND THE DANCER*

MICHAEL ROBARTES AND THE DANCER

He. Opinion is not worth a rush;
In this altar-piece the knight,
Who grips his long spear so to push
That dragon through the fading light,
Loved the lady; and it's plain
The half-dead dragon was her thought,
That every morning rose again
And dug its claws and shrieked and fought.
Could the impossible come to pass
She would have time to turn her eyes,
Her lover thought, upon the glass
And on the instant would grow wise.

She. You mean they argued.

He.   Put it so;
But bear in mind your lover's wage
Is what your looking-glass can show,
And that he will turn green with rage
At all that is not pictured there.

She. May I not put myself to college?

He. Go pluck Athene by the hair;
For what mere book can grant a knowledge
With an impassioned gravity
Appropriate to that beating breast,
That vigorous thigh, that dreaming eye?
And may the Devil take the rest.

She. And must no beautiful woman be
Learned like a man?

He.   Paul Veronese
And all his sacred company
Imagined bodies all their days
By the lagoon you love so much,
For proud, soft, ceremonious proof
That all must come to sight and touch;
While Michael Angelo's Sistine roof,
His 'Morning' and his 'Night' disclose
How sinew that has been pulled tight,
Or it may be loosened in repose,
Can rule by supernatural right
Yet be but sinew.

She.   I have heard said
There is great danger in the body.

He. Did God in portioning wine and bread
Give man His thought or His mere body?

She. My wretched dragon is perplexed.

He. I have principles to prove me right.
It follows from this Latin text
That blest souls are not composite,
And that all beautiful women may
Live in uncomposite blessedness,
And lead us to the like — if they
Will banish every thought, unless
The lineaments that please their view
When the long looking-glass is full,
Even from the foot-sole think it too.

She. They say such different things at school.

SOLOMON AND THE WITCH

AND thus declared that Arab lady:
'Last night, where under the wild moon
On grassy mattress I had laid me,
Within my arms great Solomon,
I suddenly cried out in a strange tongue
Not his, not mine.'
           Who understood
Whatever has been said, sighed, sung,
Howled, miau-d, barked, brayed, belled, yelled, cried, crowed,
Thereon replied: 'A cockerel
Crew from a blossoming apple bough
Three hundred years before the Fall,
And never crew again till now,
And would not now but that he thought,
Chance being at one with Choice at last,
All that the brigand apple brought
And this foul world were dead at last.
He that crowed out eternity
Thought to have crowed it in again.
For though love has a spider's eye
To find out some appropriate pain —
Aye, though all passion's in the glance —
For every nerve, and tests a lover
With cruelties of Choice and Chance;
And when at last that murder's over
Maybe the bride-bed brings despair,
For each an imagined image brings
And finds a real image there;
Yet the world ends when these two things,

Though several, are a single light,
When oil and wick are burned in one;
Therefore a blessed moon last night
Gave Sheba to her Solomon.'

'Yet the world stays.'
                              'If that be so,
Your cockerel found us in the wrong
Although he thought it worth a crow.
Maybe an image is too strong
Or maybe is not strong enough.'

'The night has fallen; not a sound
In the forbidden sacred grove
Unless a petal hit the ground,
Nor any human sight within it
But the crushed grass where we have lain;
And the moon is wilder every minute.
O! Solomon! let us try again.'

UNDER SATURN

Do not because this day I have grown saturnine
Imagine that lost love, inseparable from my thought
Because I have no other youth, can make me pine;
For how should I forget the wisdom that you brought,
The comfort that you made? Although my wits have gone
On a fantastic ride, my horse's flanks are spurred
By childish memories of an old cross Pollexfen,
And of a Middleton, whose name you never heard,
And of a red-haired Yeats whose looks, although he died
Before my time, seem like a vivid memory.

You heard that labouring man who had served my people.
   He said
Upon the open road, near to the Sligo quay —
No, no, not said, but cried it out — 'You have come again,
And surely after twenty years it was time to come.'
I am thinking of a child's vow sworn in vain
Never to leave that valley his fathers called their home.
   November 1919

EASTER 1916

I HAVE met them at close of day
Coming with vivid faces
From counter or desk among grey
Eighteenth-century houses.
I have passed with a nod of the head
Or polite meaningless words,
Or have lingered awhile and said
Polite meaningless words,
And thought before I had done
Of a mocking tale or a gibe
To please a companion
Around the fire at the club,
Being certain that they and I
But lived where motley is worn:
All changed, changed utterly:
A terrible beauty is born.

That woman's days were spent
In ignorant good-will,
Her nights in argument
Until her voice grew shrill.

What voice more sweet than hers
When, young and beautiful,
She rode to harriers?
This man had kept a school
And rode our wingèd horse;
This other his helper and friend
Was coming into his force;
He might have won fame in the end,
So sensitive his nature seemed,
So daring and sweet his thought.
This other man I had dreamed
A drunken, vainglorious lout.
He had done most bitter wrong
To some who are near my heart,
Yet I number him in the song;
He, too, has resigned his part
In the casual comedy;
He, too, has been changed in his turn,
Transformed utterly:
A terrible beauty is born.

Hearts with one purpose alone
Through summer and winter seem
Enchanted to a stone
To trouble the living stream.
The horse that comes from the road,
The rider, the birds that range
From cloud to tumbling cloud,
Minute by minute they change;
A shadow of cloud on the stream
Changes minute by minute;
A horse-hoof slides on the brim,
And a horse plashes within it;

The long-legged moor-hens dive,
And hens to moor-cocks call;
Minute by minute they live:
The stone's in the midst of all.

Too long a sacrifice
Can make a stone of the heart.
O when may it suffice?
That is Heaven's part, our part
To murmur name upon name,
As a mother names her child
When sleep at last has come
On limbs that had run wild.
What is it but nightfall?
No, no, not night but death;
Was it needless death after all?
For England may keep faith
For all that is done and said.
We know their dream; enough
To know they dreamed and are dead;
And what if excess of love
Bewildered them till they died?
I write it out in a verse —
MacDonagh and MacBride
And Connolly and Pearse
Now and in time to be,
Wherever green is worn,
Are changed, changed utterly:
A terrible beauty is born.

September 25, 1916

ON A POLITICAL PRISONER

She that but little patience knew,
From childhood on, had now so much
A grey gull lost its fear and flew
Down to her cell and there alit,
And there endured her fingers' touch
And from her fingers ate its bit.

Did she in touching that lone wing
Recall the years before her mind
Became a bitter, an abstract thing,
Her thought some popular enmity:
Blind and leader of the blind
Drinking the foul ditch where they lie?

When long ago I saw her ride
Under Ben Bulben to the meet,
The beauty of her country-side
With all youth's lonely wildness stirred,
She seemed to have grown clean and sweet
Like any rock-bred, sea-borne bird:

Sea-borne, or balanced on the air
When first it sprang out of the nest
Upon some lofty rock to stare
Upon the cloudy canopy,
While under its storm-beaten breast
Cried out the hollows of the sea.

TOWARDS BREAK OF DAY

WAS it the double of my dream
The woman that by me lay
Dreamed, or did we halve a dream
Under the first cold gleam of day?

I thought: 'There is a waterfall
Upon Ben Bulben side
That all my childhood counted dear;
Were I to travel far and wide
I could not find a thing so dear.'
My memories had magnified
So many times childish delight.

I would have touched it like a child
But knew my finger could but have touched
Cold stone and water. I grew wild,
Even accusing Heaven because
It had set down among its laws:
Nothing that we love over-much
Is ponderable to our touch.

I dreamed towards break of day,
The cold blown spray in my nostril.
But she that beside me lay
Had watched in bitterer sleep
The marvellous stag of Arthur,
That lofty white stag, leap
From mountain steep to steep.

DEMON AND BEAST

For certain minutes at the least
That crafty demon and that loud beast
That plague me day and night
Ran out of my sight;
Though I had long perned in the gyre,
Between my hatred and desire,
I saw my freedom won
And all laugh in the sun.

The glittering eyes in a death's head
Of old Luke Wadding's portrait said
Welcome, and the Ormondes all
Nodded upon the wall,
And even Strafford smiled as though
It made him happier to know
I understood his plan.
Now that the loud beast ran
There was no portrait in the Gallery
But beckoned to sweet company,
For all men's thoughts grew clear
Being dear as mine are dear.

But soon a tear-drop started up,
For aimless joy had made me stop
Beside the little lake
To watch a white gull take
A bit of bread thrown up into the air;
Now gyring down and perning there
He splashed where an absurd
Portly green-pated bird
Shook off the water from his back;

Being no more demoniac
A stupid happy creature
Could rouse my whole nature.

Yet I am certain as can be
That every natural victory
Belongs to beast or demon,
That never yet had freeman
Right mastery of natural things,
And that mere growing old, that brings
Chilled blood, this sweetness brought;
Yet have no dearer thought
Than that I may find out a way
To make it linger half a day.

O what a sweetness strayed
Through barren Thebaid,
Or by the Mareotic sea
When that exultant Anthony
And twice a thousand more
Starved upon the shore
And withered to a bag of bones!
What had the Caesars but their thrones?

THE SECOND COMING

TURNING and turning in the widening gyre
The falcon cannot hear the falconer;
Things fall apart; the centre cannot hold;
Mere anarchy is loosed upon the world,
The blood-dimmed tide is loosed, and everywhere
The ceremony of innocence is drowned;

The best lack all conviction, while the worst
Are full of passionate intensity.

Surely some revelation is at hand;
Surely the Second Coming is at hand.
The Second Coming! Hardly are those words out
When a vast image out of *Spiritus Mundi*
Troubles my sight: somewhere in sands of the desert
A shape with lion body and the head of a man,
A gaze blank and pitiless as the sun,
Is moving its slow thighs, while all about it
Reel shadows of the indignant desert birds.
The darkness drops again; but now I know
That twenty centuries of stony sleep
Were vexed to nightmare by a rocking cradle,
And what rough beast, its hour come round at last,
Slouches towards Bethlehem to be born?

A PRAYER FOR MY DAUGHTER

ONCE more the storm is howling, and half hid
Under this cradle-hood and coverlid
My child sleeps on. There is no obstacle
But Gregory's wood and one bare hill
Whereby the haystack- and roof-levelling wind,
Bred on the Atlantic, can be stayed;
And for an hour I have walked and prayed
Because of the great gloom that is in my mind.

I have walked and prayed for this young child an hour
And heard the sea-wind scream upon the tower,
And under the arches of the bridge, and scream
In the elms above the flooded stream;

Imagining in excited reverie
That the future years had come,
Dancing to a frenzied drum,
Out of the murderous innocence of the sea.

May she be granted beauty and yet not
Beauty to make a stranger's eye distraught,
Or hers before a looking-glass, for such,
Being made beautiful overmuch,
Consider beauty a sufficient end,
Lose natural kindness and maybe
The heart-revealing intimacy
That chooses right, and never find a friend.

Helen being chosen found life flat and dull
And later had much trouble from a fool,
While that great Queen, that rose out of the spray,
Being fatherless could have her way
Yet chose a bandy-leggèd smith for man.
It's certain that fine women eat
A crazy salad with their meat
Whereby the Horn of Plenty is undone.

In courtesy I'd have her chiefly learned;
Hearts are not had as a gift but hearts are earned
By those that are not entirely beautiful;
Yet many, that have played the fool
For beauty's very self, has charm made wise,
And many a poor man that has roved,
Loved and thought himself beloved,
From a glad kindness cannot take his eyes.

May she become a flourishing hidden tree
That all her thoughts may like the linnet be,
And have no business but dispensing round
Their magnanimities of sound,
Nor but in merriment begin a chase,
Nor but in merriment a quarrel.
O may she live like some green laurel
Rooted in one dear perpetual place.

My mind, because the minds that I have loved,
The sort of beauty that I have approved,
Prosper but little, has dried up of late,
Yet knows that to be choked with hate
May well be of all evil chances chief.
If there's no hatred in a mind
Assault and battery of the wind
Can never tear the linnet from the leaf.

An intellectual hatred is the worst,
So let her think opinions are accursed.
Have I not seen the loveliest woman born
Out of the mouth of Plenty's horn,
Because of her opinionated mind
Barter that horn and every good
By quiet natures understood
For an old bellows full of angry wind?

Considering that, all hatred driven hence,
The soul recovers radical innocence
And learns at last that it is self-delighting,
Self-appeasing, self-affrighting,

And that its own sweet will is Heaven's will;
She can, though every face should scowl
And every windy quarter howl
Or every bellows burst, be happy still.

And may her bridegroom bring her to a house
Where all's accustomed, ceremonious;
For arrogance and hatred are the wares
Peddled in the thoroughfares.
How but in custom and in ceremony
Are innocence and beauty born?
Ceremony's a name for the rich horn,
And custom for the spreading laurel tree.

June 1919

A MEDITATION IN TIME OF WAR

FOR one throb of the artery,
While on that old grey stone I sat
Under the old wind-broken tree,
I knew that One is animate,
Mankind inanimate fantasy.

From *THE TOWER*

SAILING TO BYZANTIUM

I

THAT is no country for old men. The young
In one another's arms, birds in the trees
— Those dying generations — at their song,
The salmon-falls, the mackerel-crowded seas,
Fish, flesh, or fowl, commend all summer long
Whatever is begotten, born, and dies.
Caught in that sensual music all neglect
Monuments of unageing intellect.

II

An aged man is but a paltry thing,
A tattered coat upon a stick, unless
Soul clap its hands and sing, and louder sing
For every tatter in its mortal dress,
Nor is there singing school but studying
Monuments of its own magnificence;
And therefore I have sailed the seas and come
To the holy city of Byzantium.

III

O sages standing in God's holy fire
As in the gold mosaic of a wall,
Come from the holy fire, perne in a gyre,
And be the singing-masters of my soul.

Consume my heart away; sick with desire
And fastened to a dying animal
It knows not what it is; and gather me
Into the artifice of eternity.

IV

Once out of nature I shall never take
My bodily form from any natural thing,
But such a form as Grecian goldsmiths make
Of hammered gold and gold enamelling
To keep a drowsy Emperor awake;
Or set upon a golden bough to sing
To lords and ladies of Byzantium
Of what is past, or passing, or to come.

1927

THE TOWER

I

WHAT shall I do with this absurdity —
O heart, O troubled heart — this caricature,
Decrepit age that has been tied to me
As to a dog's tail?
                    Never had I more
Excited, passionate, fantastical
Imagination, nor an ear and eye
That more expected the impossible —
No, not in boyhood when with rod and fly,
Or the humbler worm, I climbed Ben Bulben's back
And had the livelong summer day to spend.

It seems that I must bid the Muse go pack,
Choose Plato and Plotinus for a friend
Until imagination, ear and eye,
Can be content with argument and deal
In abstract things; or be derided by
A sort of battered kettle at the heel.

II

I pace upon the battlements and stare
On the foundations of a house, or where
Tree, like a sooty finger, starts from the earth;
And send imagination forth
Under the day's declining beam, and call
Images and memories
From ruin or from ancient trees,
For I would ask a question of them all.

Beyond that ridge lived Mrs. French, and once
When every silver candlestick or sconce
Lit up the dark mahogany and the wine,
A serving-man, that could divine
That most respected lady's every wish,
Ran and with the garden shears
Clipped an insolent farmer's ears
And brought them in a little covered dish.

Some few remembered still when I was young
A peasant girl commended by a song,
Who'd lived somewhere upon that rocky place,
And praised the colour of her face,
And had the greater joy in praising her,
Remembering that, if walked she there,
Farmers jostled at the fair
So great a glory did the song confer.

And certain men, being maddened by those rhymes,
Or else by toasting her a score of times,
Rose from the table and declared it right
To test their fancy by their sight;
But they mistook the brightness of the moon
For the prosaic light of day —
Music had driven their wits astray —
And one was drowned in the great bog of Cloone.

Strange, but the man who made the song was blind;
Yet, now I have considered it, I find
That nothing strange; the tragedy began
With Homer that was a blind man,
And Helen has all living hearts betrayed.
O may the moon and sunlight seem
One inextricable beam,
For if I triumph I must make men mad.

And I myself created Hanrahan
And drove him drunk or sober through the dawn
From somewhere in the neighbouring cottages.
Caught by an old man's juggleries
He stumbled, tumbled, fumbled to and fro
And had but broken knees for hire
And horrible splendour of desire;
I thought it all out twenty years ago:

Good fellows shuffled cards in an old bawn;
And when that ancient ruffian's turn was on
He so bewitched the cards under his thumb
That all but the one card became
A pack of hounds and not a pack of cards,
And that he changed into a hare.

Hanrahan rose in frenzy there
And followed up those baying creatures towards —

O towards I have forgotten what — enough!
I must recall a man that neither love
Nor music nor an enemy's clipped ear
Could, he was so harried, cheer;
A figure that has grown so fabulous
There's not a neighbour left to say
When he finished his dog's day:
An ancient bankrupt master of this house.

Before that ruin came, for centuries,
Rough men-at-arms, cross-gartered to the knees
Or shod in iron, climbed the narrow stairs,
And certain men-at-arms there were
Whose images, in the Great Memory stored,
Come with loud cry and panting breast
To break upon a sleeper's rest
While their great wooden dice beat on the board.

As I would question all, come all who can;
Come old, necessitous, half-mounted man;
And bring beauty's blind rambling celebrant;
The red man the juggler sent
Through God-forsaken meadows; Mrs. French,
Gifted with so fine an ear;
The man drowned in a bog's mire,
When mocking Muses chose the country wench.

Did all old men and women, rich and poor,
Who trod upon these rocks or passed this door,
Whether in public or in secret rage
As I do now against old age?

But I have found an answer in those eyes
That are impatient to be gone;
Go therefore; but leave Hanrahan,
For I need all his mighty memories.

Old lecher with a love on every wind,
Bring up out of that deep considering mind
All that you have discovered in the grave,
For it is certain that you have
Reckoned up every unforeknown, unseeing
Plunge, lured by a softening eye,
Or by a touch or a sigh,
Into the labyrinth of another's being;

Does the imagination dwell the most
Upon a woman won or woman lost?
If on the lost, admit you turned aside
From a great labyrinth out of pride,
Cowardice, some silly over-subtle thought
Or anything called conscience once;
And that if memory recur, the sun's
Under eclipse and the day blotted out.

III

It is time that I wrote my will;
I choose upstanding men
That climb the streams until
The fountain leap, and at dawn
Drop their cast at the side
Of dripping stone; I declare
They shall inherit my pride,

The pride of people that were
Bound neither to Cause nor to State,
Neither to slaves that were spat on,
Nor to the tyrants that spat,
The people of Burke and of Grattan
That gave, though free to refuse —
Pride, like that of the morn,
When the headlong light is loose,
Or that of the fabulous horn,
Or that of the sudden shower
When all streams are dry,
Or that of the hour
When the swan must fix his eye
Upon a fading gleam,
Float out upon a long
Last reach of glittering stream
And there sing his last song.
And I declare my faith:
I mock Plotinus' thought
And cry in Plato's teeth,
Death and life were not
Till man made up the whole,
Made lock, stock and barrel
Out of his bitter soul,
Aye, sun and moon and star, all,
And further add to that
That, being dead, we rise,
Dream and so create
Translunar Paradise.
I have prepared my peace
With learned Italian things
And the proud stones of Greece,
Poet's imaginings

And memories of love,
Memories of the words of women,
All those things whereof
Man makes a superhuman
Mirror-resembling dream.

As at the loophole there
The daws chatter and scream,
And drop twigs layer upon layer.
When they have mounted up,
The mother bird will rest
On their hollow top,
And so warm her wild nest.

I leave both faith and pride
To young upstanding men
Climbing the mountain-side,
That under bursting dawn
They may drop a fly;
Being of that metal made
Till it was broken by
This sedentary trade.

Now shall I make my soul,
Compelling it to study
In a learned school
Till the wreck of body,
Slow decay of blood,
Testy delirium
Or dull decrepitude,
Or what worse evil come —
The death of friends, or death
Of every brilliant eye
That made a catch in the breath —

Seem but the clouds of the sky
When the horizon fades:
Or a bird's sleepy cry
Among the deepening shades.

1926

MEDITATIONS IN TIME OF CIVIL WAR

I

Ancestral Houses

SURELY among a rich man's flowering lawns,
Amid the rustle of his planted hills,
Life overflows without ambitious pains;
And rains down life until the basin spills,
And mounts more dizzy high the more it rains
As though to choose whatever shape it wills
And never stoop to a mechanical
Or servile shape, at others' beck and call.

Mere dreams, mere dreams! Yet Homer had not sung
Had he not found it certain beyond dreams
That out of life's own self-delight had sprung
The abounding glittering jet; though now it seems
As if some marvellous empty sea-shell flung
Out of the obscure dark of the rich streams,
And not a fountain, were the symbol which
Shadows the inherited glory of the rich.

Some violent bitter man, some powerful man
Called architect and artist in, that they,
Bitter and violent men, might rear in stone
The sweetness that all longed for night and day,

The gentleness none there had ever known;
But when the master's buried mice can play,
And maybe the great-grandson of that house,
For all its bronze and marble, 's but a mouse.

O what if gardens where the peacock strays
With delicate feet upon old terraces,
Or else all Juno from an urn displays
Before the indifferent garden deities;
O what if levelled lawns and gravelled ways
Where slippered Contemplation finds his ease
And Childhood a delight for every sense,
But take our greatness with our violence?

What if the glory of escutcheoned doors,
And buildings that a haughtier age designed,
The pacing to and fro on polished floors
Amid great chambers and long galleries, lined
With famous portraits of our ancestors;
What if those things the greatest of mankind
Consider most to magnify, or to bless,
But take our greatness with our bitterness?

II
My House

An ancient bridge, and a more ancient tower,
A farmhouse that is sheltered by its wall,
An acre of stony ground,
Where the symbolic rose can break in flower,
Old ragged elms, old thorns innumerable,
The sound of the rain or sound
Of every wind that blows;

The stilted water-hen
Crossing stream again
Scared by the splashing of a dozen cows;

A winding stair, a chamber arched with stone,
A grey stone fireplace with an open hearth,
A candle and written page.
Il Penseroso's Platonist toiled on
In some like chamber, shadowing forth
How the daemonic rage
Imagined everything.
Benighted travellers
From markers and from fairs
Have seen his midnight candle glimmering.

Two men have founded here. A man-at-arms
Gathered a score of horse and spent his days
In this tumultuous spot,
Where through long wars and sudden night alarms
His dwindling score and he seemed castaways
Forgetting and forgot;
And I, that after me
My bodily heirs may find,
To exalt a lonely mind,
Befitting emblems of adversity.

III
My Table

Two heavy trestles, and a board
Where Sato's gift, a changeless sword,
By pen and paper lies,
That it may moralise
My days out of their aimlessness.

A bit of an embroidered dress
Covers its wooden sheath.
Chaucer had not drawn breath
When it was forged. In Sato's house,
Curved like new moon, moon-luminous,
It lay five hundred years.
Yet if no change appears
No moon; only an aching heart
Conceives a changeless work of art.
Our learned men have urged
That when and where 'twas forged
A marvellous accomplishment,
In painting or in pottery, went
From father unto son
And through the centuries ran
And seemed unchanging like the sword.
Soul's beauty being most adored,
Men and their business took
The soul's unchanging look;
For the most rich inheritor,
Knowing that none could pass Heaven's door
That loved inferior art,
Had such an aching heart
That he, although a country's talk
For silken clothes and stately walk,
Had waking wits; it seemed
Juno's peacock screamed.

IV

My Descendants

Having inherited a vigorous mind
From my old fathers, I must nourish dreams
And leave a woman and a man behind
As vigorous of mind, and yet it seems
Life scarce can cast a fragrance on the wind,
Scarce spread a glory to the morning beams,
But the torn petals strew the garden plot;
And there's but common greenness after that.

And what if my descendants lose the flower
Through natural declension of the soul,
Through too much business with the passing hour,
Through too much play, or marriage with a fool?
May this laborious stair and this stark tower
Become a roofless ruin that the owl
May build in the cracked masonry and cry
Her desolation to the desolate sky.

The Primum Mobile that fashioned us
Has made the very owls in circles move;
And I, that count myself most prosperous,
Seeing that love and friendship are enough,
For an old neighbour's friendship chose the house
And decked and altered it for a girl's love,
And know whatever flourish and decline
These stones remain their monument and mine.

V

The Road at My Door

An affable Irregular,
A heavily-built Falstaffian man,
Comes cracking jokes of civil war
As though to die by gunshot were
The finest play under the sun.

A brown Lieutenant and his men,
Half dressed in national uniform,
Stand at my door, and I complain
Of the foul weather, hail and rain,
A pear-tree broken by the storm.

I count those feathered balls of soot
The moor-hen guides upon the stream,
To silence the envy in my thought;
And turn towards my chamber, caught
In the cold snows of a dream.

IV

The Stare's Nest by My Window

The bees build in the crevices
Of loosening masonry, and there
The mother birds bring grubs and flies.
My wall is loosening; honey-bees,
Come build in the empty house of the stare.

We are closed in, and the key is turned
On our uncertainty; somewhere
A man is killed, or a house burned,

Yet no clear fact to be discerned:
Come build in the empty house of the stare.

A barricade of stone or of wood;
Some fourteen days of civil war;
Last night they trundled down the road
That dead young soldier in his blood:
Come build in the empty house of the stare.

We had fed the heart on fantasies,
The heart's grown brutal from the fare;
More substance in our enmities
Than in our love; O honey-bees,
Come build in the empty house of the stare.

VII

*I see Phantoms of Hatred and of the Heart's Fullness
and of the Coming Emptiness*

I climb to the tower-top and lean upon broken stone,
A mist that is like blown snow is sweeping over all,
Valley, river, and elms, under the light of a moon
That seems unlike itself, that seems unchangeable,
A glittering sword out of the east. A puff of wind
And those white glimmering fragments of the mist sweep by.
Frenzies bewilder, reveries perturb the mind;
Monstrous familiar images swim to the mind's eye.

'Vengeance upon the murderers,' the cry goes up,
'Vengeance for Jacques Molay.' In cloud-pale rags, or in lace,
The rage-driven, rage-tormented, and rage-hungry troop,
Trooper belabouring trooper, biting at arm or at face,

Plunges towards nothing, arms and fingers spreading wide
For the embrace of nothing; and I, my wits astray
Because of all that senseless tumult, all but cried
For vengeance on the murderers of Jacques Molay.

Their legs long, delicate and slender, aquamarine their eyes,
Magical unicorns bear ladies on their backs.
The ladies close their musing eyes. No prophecies,
Remembered out of Babylonian almanacs,
Have closed the ladies' eyes, their minds are but a pool
Where even longing drowns under its own excess;
Nothing but stillness can remain when hearts are full
Of their own sweetness, bodies of their loveliness.

The cloud-pale unicorns, the eyes of aquamarine,
The quivering half-closed eyelids, the rags of cloud or of lace,
Or eyes that rage has brightened, arms it has made lean,
Give place to an indifferent multitude, give place
To brazen hawks. Nor self-delighting reverie,
Nor hate of what's to come, nor pity for what's gone,
Nothing but grip of claw, and the eye's complacency,
The innumerable clanging wings that have put out the moon.

I turn away and shut the door, and on the stair
Wonder how many times I could have proved my worth
In something that all others understand or share;
But O! ambitious heart, had such a proof drawn forth
A company of friends, a conscience set at ease,
It had but made us pine the more. The abstract joy,
The half-read wisdom of daemonic images,
Suffice the ageing man as once the growing boy.

  1923

NINETEEN HUNDRED AND NINETEEN

I

MANY ingenious lovely things are gone
That seemed sheer miracle to the multitude,
Protected from the circle of the moon
That pitches common things about. There stood
Amid the ornamental bronze and stone
An ancient image made of olive wood —
And gone are Phidias' famous ivories
And all the golden grasshoppers and bees.

We too had many pretty toys when young:
A law indifferent to blame or praise,
To bribe or threat; habits that made old wrong
Melt down, as it were wax in the sun's rays;
Public opinion ripening for so long
We thought it would outlive all future days.
O what fine thought we had because we thought
That the worst rogues and rascals had died out.

All teeth were drawn, all ancient tricks unlearned,
And a great army but a showy thing;
What matter that no cannon had been turned
Into a ploughshare? Parliament and king
Thought that unless a little powder burned
The trumpeters might burst with trumpeting
And yet it lack all glory; and perchance
The guardsmen's drowsy chargers would not prance.

Now days are dragon-ridden, the nightmare
Rides upon sleep: a drunken soldiery
Can leave the mother, murdered at her door,
To crawl in her own blood, and go scot-free;
The night can sweat with terror as before
We pieced our thoughts into philosophy,
And planned to bring the world under a rule,
Who are but weasels fighting in a hole.

He who can read the signs nor sink unmanned
Into the half-deceit of some intoxicant
From shallow wits; who knows no work can stand,
Whether health, wealth or peace of mind were spent
On master-work of intellect or hand,
No honour leave its mighty monument,
Has but one comfort left: all triumph would
But break upon his ghostly solitude.

But is there any comfort to be found?
Man is in love and loves what vanishes,
What more is there to say? That country round
None dared admit, if such a thought were his,
Incendiary or bigot could be found
To burn that stump on the Acropolis,
Or break in bits the famous ivories
Or traffic in the grasshoppers or bees.

II

When Loie Fuller's Chinese dancers enwound
A shining web, a floating ribbon of cloth,
It seemed that a dragon of air
Had fallen among dancers, had whirled them round

Or hurried them off on its own furious path;
So the Platonic Year
Whirls out new right and wrong,
Whirls in the old instead;
All men are dancers and their tread
Goes to the barbarous clangour of a gong.

III

Some moralist or mythological poet
Compares the solitary soul to a swan;
I am satisfied with that,
Satisfied if a troubled mirror show it,
Before that brief gleam of its life be gone,
An image of its state;
The wings half spread for flight,
The breast thrust out in pride
Whether to play, or to ride
Those winds that clamour of approaching night,

A man in his own secret meditation
Is lost amid the labyrinth that he has made
In art or politics;
Some Platonist affirms that in the station
Where we should cast off body and trade
The ancient habit sticks,
And that if our works could
But vanish with our breath
That were a lucky death,
For triumph can but mar our solitude.

The swan has leaped into the desolate heaven:
That image can bring wildness, bring a rage
To end all things, to end

What my laborious life imagined, even
The half-imagined, the half-written page;
O but we dreamed to mend
Whatever mischief seemed
To afflict mankind, but now
That winds of winter blow
Learn that we were crack-pated when we dreamed.

IV

We, who seven years ago
Talked of honour and of truth,
Shriek with pleasure if we show
The weasel's twist, the weasel's tooth.

V

Come let us mock at the great
That had such burdens on the mind
And toiled so hard and late
To leave some monument behind,
Nor thought of the levelling wind.

Come let us mock at the wise;
With all those calendars whereon
They fixed old aching eyes,
They never saw how seasons run,
And now but gape at the sun.

Come let us mock at the good
That fancied goodness might be gay,
And sick of solitude
Might proclaim a holiday:
Wind shrieked — and where are they?

Mock mockers after that
That would not lift a hand maybe
To help good, wise or great
To bar that foul storm out, for we
Traffic in mockery.

VI

Violence upon the roads: violence of horses;
Some few have handsome riders, are garlanded
On delicate sensitive ear or tossing mane,
But wearied running round and round in their courses
All break and vanish, and evil gathers head:
Herodias' daughters have returned again,
A sudden blast of dusty wind and after
Thunder of feet, tumult of images,
Their purpose in the labyrinth of the wind;
And should some crazy hand dare touch a daughter
All turn with amorous cries, or angry cries,
According to the wind, for all are blind.
But now wind drops, dust settles; thereupon
There lurches past, his great eyes without thought
Under the shadow of stupid straw-pale locks,
That insolent fiend Robert Artisson
To whom the love-lorn Lady Kyteler brought
Bronzed peacock feathers, red combs of her cocks.

1919

THE WHEEL

THROUGH winter-time we call on spring,
And through the spring on summer call,
And when abounding hedges ring
Declare that winter's best of all;

And after that there's nothing good
Because the spring-time has not come —
Nor know that what disturbs our blood
Is but its longing for the tomb.

THE NEW FACES

If you, that have grown old, were the first dead,
Neither catalpa tree nor scented lime
Should hear my living feet, nor would I tread
Where we wrought that shall break the teeth of Time.
Let the new faces play what tricks they will
In the old rooms; night can outbalance day,
Our shadows rove the garden gravel still,
The living seem more shadowy than they.

TWO SONGS FROM A PLAY

I

I saw a staring virgin stand
Where holy Dionysus died,
And tear the heart out of his side,
And lay the heart upon her hand
And bear that beating heart away;
And then did all the Muses sing
Of Magnus Annus at the spring,
As though God's death were but a play.

Another Troy must rise and set,
Another lineage feed the crow,
Another Argo's painted prow
Drive to a flashier bauble yet.
The Roman Empire stood appalled:
It dropped the reins of peace and war
When that fierce virgin and her Star
Out of the fabulous darkness called.

II

In pity for man's darkening thought
He walked that room and issued thence
In Galilean turbulence;
The Babylonian starlight brought
A fabulous, formless darkness in;
Odour of blood when Christ was slain
Made all Platonic tolerance vain
And vain all Doric discipline.

Everything that man esteems
Endures a moment or a day.
Love's pleasure drives his love away,
The painter's brush consumes his dreams;
The herald's cry, the soldier's tread
Exhaust his glory and his might:
Whatever flames upon the night
Man's own resinous heart has fed.

LEDA AND THE SWAN

A SUDDEN blow: the great wings beating still
Above the staggering girl, her thighs caressed
By the dark webs, her nape caught in his bill,
He holds her helpless breast upon his breast.

How can those terrified vague fingers push
The feathered glory from her loosening thighs?
And how can body, laid in that white rush,
But feel the strange heart beating where it lies?

A shudder in the loins engenders there
The broken wall, the burning roof and tower
And Agamemnon dead.
                              Being so caught up,
So mastered by the brute blood of the air,
Did she put on his knowledge with his power
Before the indifferent beak could let her drop?
    1923

AMONG SCHOOL CHILDREN

I

I WALK through the long schoolroom questioning;
A kind old nun in a white hood replies;
The children learn to cipher and to sing,
To study reading-books and histories,
To cut and sew, be neat in everything
In the best modern way — the children's eyes
In momentary wonder stare upon
A sixty-year-old smiling public man.

II

I dream of a Ledaean body, bent
Above a sinking fire, a tale that she
Told of a harsh reproof, or trivial event
That changed some childish day to tragedy —
Told, and it seemed that our two natures blent
Into a sphere from youthful sympathy,
Or else, to alter Plato's parable,
Into the yolk and white of the one shell.

III

And thinking of that fit of grief or rage
I look upon one child or t'other there
And wonder if she stood so at that age —
For even daughters of the swan can share
Something of every paddler's heritage —
And had that colour upon cheek or hair,
And thereupon my heart is driven wild:
She stands before me as a living child.

IV

Her present image floats into the mind —
Did Quattrocento finger fashion it
Hollow of cheek as though it drank the wind
And took a mess of shadows for its meat?
And I though never of Ledaean kind
Had pretty plumage once — enough of that,
Better to smile on all that smile, and show
There is a comfortable kind of old scarecrow.

V

What youthful mother, a shape upon her lap
Honey of generation had betrayed,
And that must sleep, shriek, struggle to escape
As recollection or the drug decide,
Would think her son, did she but see that shape
With sixty or more winters on its head,
A compensation for the pang of his birth,
Or the uncertainty of his setting forth?

VI

Plato thought nature but a spume that plays
Upon a ghostly paradigm of things;
Solider Aristotle played the taws
Upon the bottom of a king of kings;
World-famous golden-thighed Pythagoras
Fingered upon a fiddle-stick or strings
What a star sang and careless Muses heard:
Old clothes upon old sticks to scare a bird.

VII

Both nuns and mothers worship images,
But those the candles light are not as those
That animate a mother's reveries,
But keep a marble or a bronze repose.
And yet they too break hearts — O Presences
That passion, piety or affection knows,
And that all heavenly glory symbolise —
O self-born mockers of man's enterprise;

VIII

Labour is blossoming or dancing where
The body is not bruised to pleasure soul,
Nor beauty born out of its own despair,
Nor blear-eyed wisdom out of midnight oil.
O chestnut-tree, great-rooted blossomer,
Are you the leaf, the blossom or the bole?
O body swayed to music, O brightening glance,
How can we know the dancer from the dance?

COLONUS' PRAISE

(From 'Oedipus at Colonus')

Chorus. Come praise Colonus' horses, and come praise
　　The wine-dark of the wood's intricacies,
　　The nightingale that deafens daylight there,
　　If daylight ever visit where,
　　Unvisited by tempest or by sun,
　　Immortal ladies tread the ground
　　Dizzy with harmonious sound,
　　Semele's lad a gay companion.

　　And yonder in the gymnasts' garden thrives
　　The self-sown, self-begotten shape that gives
　　Athenian intellect its mastery,
　　Even the grey-leaved olive-tree
　　Miracle-bred out of the living stone;
　　Nor accident of peace nor war
　　Shall wither that old marvel, for
　　The great grey-eyed Athene stares thereon.

Who comes into this country, and has come
Where golden crocus and narcissus bloom,
Where the Great Mother, mourning for her daughter
And beauty-drunken by the water
Glittering among grey-leaved olive-trees,
Has plucked a flower and sung her loss;
Who finds abounding Cephisus
Has found the loveliest spectacle there is.

Because this country has a pious mind
And so remembers that when all mankind
But trod the road, or splashed about the shore,
Poseidon gave it bit and oar,
Every Colonus lad or lass discourses
Of that oar and of that bit;
Summer and winter, day and night,
Of horses and horses of the sea, white horses.

OWEN AHERNE AND HIS DANCERS

I

A STRANGE thing surely that my Heart, when love had come
    unsought
Upon the Norman upland or in that poplar shade,
Should find no burden but itself and yet should be worn out.
It could not bear that burden and therefore it went mad.

The south wind brought it longing, and the east wind despair,
The west wind made it pitiful, and the north wind afraid.
It feared to give its love a hurt with all the tempest there;
It feared the hurt that she could give and therefore it went
    mad.

I can exchange opinion with any neighbouring mind,
I have as healthy flesh and blood as any rhymer's had,
But O! my Heart could bear no more when the upland
    caught the wind;
I ran, I ran, from my love's side because my Heart went mad.

II

The Heart behind its rib laughed out. 'You have called me
    mad,' it said,
'Because I made you turn away and run from that young
    child;
How could she mate with fifty years that was so wildly
    bred?
Let the cage bird and the cage bird mate and the wild bird
    mate in the wild.'

'You but imagine lies all day, O murderer,' I replied.
'And all those lies have but one end, poor wretches to betray;
I did not find in any cage the woman at my side.
O but her heart would break to learn my thoughts are far
    away.'

'Speak all your mind,' my Heart sang out, 'speak all your
    mind; who cares,
Now that your tongue cannot persuade the child till she
    mistake
Her childish gratitude for love and match your fifty years?
O let her choose a young man now and all for his wild sake.'

A MAN YOUNG AND OLD

I

First Love

THOUGH nurtured like the sailing moon
In beauty's murderous brood,
She walked awhile and blushed awhile
And on my pathway stood
Until I thought her body bore
A heart of flesh and blood.

But since I laid a hand thereon
And found a heart of stone
I have attempted many things
And not a thing is done,
For every hand is lunatic
That travels on the moon.

She smiled and that transfigured me
And left me but a lout,
Maundering here, and maundering there,
Emptier of thought
Than the heavenly circuit of its stars
When the moon sails out.

III

The Mermaid

A mermaid found a swimming lad,
Picked him for her own,
Pressed her body to his body,
Laughed; and plunging down
Forgot in cruel happiness
That even lovers drown.

VI

His Memories

We should be hidden from their eyes,
Being but holy shows
And bodies broken like a thorn
Whereon the bleak north blows,
To think of buried Hector
And that none living knows.

The women take so little stock
In what I do or say
They'd sooner leave their cosseting
To hear a jackass bray;
My arms are like the twisted thorn
And yet there beauty lay;

The first of all the tribe lay there
And did such pleasure take —
She who had brought great Hector down
And put all Troy to wreck —
That she cried into this ear,
'Strike me if I shriek.'

VIII

Summer and Spring

We sat under an old thorn-tree
And talked away the night,
Told all that had been said or done
Since first we saw the light,

And when we talked of growing up
Knew that we'd halved a soul
And fell the one in t'other's arms
That we might make it whole;
Then Peter had a murdering look,
For it seemed that he and she
Had spoken of their childish days
Under that very tree.
O what a bursting out there was,
And what a blossoming,
When we had all the summer-time
And she had all the spring!

IX

The Secrets of the Old

I have old women's secrets now
That had those of the young;
Madge tells me what I dared not think
When my blood was strong,
And what had drowned a lover once
Sounds like an old song.

Though Margery is stricken dumb
If thrown in Madge's way,
We three make up a solitude;
For none alive to-day
Can know the stories that we know
Or say the things we say:

How such a man pleased women most
Of all that are gone,

How such a pair loved many years
And such a pair but one,
Stories of the bed of straw
Or the bed of down.

XI

From 'Oedipus at Colonus'

Endure what life God gives and ask no longer span;
Cease to remember the delights of youth, travel-wearied aged
man;
Delight becomes death-longing if all longing else be vain.

Even from that delight memory treasures so,
Death, despair, division of families, all entanglements of
mankind grow,
As that old wandering beggar and these God-hated children
know.

In the long echoing street the laughing dancers throng,
The bride is carried to the bridegroom's chamber through
torchlight and tumultuous song;
I celebrate the silent kiss that ends short life or long.

Never to have lived is best, ancient writers say;
Never to have drawn the breath of life, never to have looked
into the eye of day;
The second best's a gay goodnight and quickly turn away.

ALL SOULS' NIGHT

Epilogue to 'A Vision'

MIDNIGHT has come, and the great Christ Church Bell
And many a lesser bell sound through the room;
And it is All Souls' Night,
And two long glasses brimmed with muscatel
Bubble upon the table. A ghost may come;
For it is a ghost's right,
His element is so fine
Being sharpened by his death,
To drink from the wine-breath
While our gross palates drink from the whole wine.

I need some mind that, if the cannon sound
From every quarter of the world, can stay
Wound in mind's pondering
As mummies in the mummy-cloth are wound;
Because I have a marvellous thing to say,
A certain marvellous thing
None but the living mock,
Though not for sober ear;
It may be all that hear
Should laugh and weep an hour upon the clock.

Horton's the first I call. He loved strange thought
And knew that sweet extremity of pride
That's called platonic love,
And that to such a pitch of passion wrought
Nothing could bring him, when his lady died,
Anodyne for his love.

Words were but wasted breath;
One dear hope had he:
The inclemency
Of that or the next winter would be death.

Two thoughts were so mixed up I could not tell
Whether of her or God he thought the most,
But think that his mind's eye,
When upward turned, on one sole image fell;
And that a slight companionable ghost,
Wild with divinity,
Had so lit up the whole
Immense miraculous house
The Bible promised us,
It seemed a gold-fish swimming in a bowl.

On Florence Emery I call the next,
Who finding the first wrinkles on a face
Admired and beautiful,
And knowing that the future would be vexed
With 'minished beauty, multiplied commonplace,
Preferred to teach a school
Away from neighbour or friend,
Among dark skins, and there
Permit foul years to wear
Hidden from eyesight to the unnoticed end.

Before that end much had she ravelled out
From a discourse in figurative speech
By some learned Indian
On the soul's journey. How it is whirled about,
Wherever the orbit of the moon can reach,
Until it plunge into the sun;

And there, free and yet fast,
Being both Chance and Choice,
Forget its broken toys
And sink into its own delight at last.

And I call up MacGregor from the grave,
For in my first hard springtime we were friends,
Although of late estranged.
I thought him half a lunatic, half knave,
And told him so, but friendship never ends;
And what if mind seem changed,
And it seem changed with the mind,
When thoughts rise up unbid
On generous things that he did
And I grow half contented to be blind!

He had much industry at setting out,
Much boisterous courage, before loneliness
Had driven him crazed;
For meditations upon unknown thought
Make human intercourse grow less and less;
They are neither paid nor praised.
But he'd object to the host,
The glass because my glass;
A ghost-lover he was
And may have grown more arrogant being a ghost.

But names are nothing. What matter who it be,
So that his elements have grown so fine
The fume of muscatel
Can give his sharpened palate ecstasy
No living man can drink from the whole wine.
I have mummy truths to tell
Whereat the living mock,

Though not for sober ear,
For maybe all that hear
Should laugh and weep an hour upon the clock.

Such thought — such thought have I that hold it tight
Till meditation master all its parts,
Nothing can stay my glance
Until that glance run in the world's despite
To where the damned have howled away their hearts,
And where the blessed dance;
Such thought, that in it bound
I need no other thing,
Wound in mind's wandering
As mummies in the mummy-cloth are wound.

Oxford, 1920

From *THE WINDING STAIR AND OTHER POEMS*

IN MEMORY OF EVA GORE-BOOTH AND CON MARKIEWICZ

THE light of evening, Lissadell,
Great windows, open to the south,
Two girls in silk kimonos, both
Beautiful, one a gazelle.
But a raving autumn shears
Blossom from the summer's wreath;
The older is condemned to death,
Pardoned, drags out lonely years
Conspiring among the ignorant.
I know not what the younger dreams —
Some vague Utopia — and she seems,
When withered old and skeleton-gaunt,
An image of such politics.
Many a time I think to seek
One or the other out and speak
Of that old Georgian mansion, mix
Pictures of the mind, recall
That table and the talk of youth,
Two girls in silk kimonos, both
Beautiful, one a gazelle.

Dear shadows, now you know it all,
All the folly of a fight
With a common wrong or right.
The innocent and the beautiful
Have no enemy but time;

Arise and bid me strike a match
And strike another till time catch;
Should the conflagration climb,
Run till all the sages know.
We the great gazebo built,
They convicted us of guilt;
Bid me strike a match and blow.

October 1927

DEATH

NOR dread nor hope attend
A dying animal;
A man awaits his end
Dreading and hoping all;
Many times he died,
Many times rose again.
A great man in his pride
Confronting murderous men
Casts derision upon
Supersession of breath;
He knows death to the bone —
Man has created death.

A DIALOGUE OF SELF AND SOUL

I

My Soul. I summon to the winding ancient stair;
Set all your mind upon the steep ascent,
Upon the broken, crumbling battlement,
Upon the breathless starlit air,

Upon the star that marks the hidden pole;
Fix every wandering thought upon
That quarter where all thought is done:
Who can distinguish darkness from the soul?

My Self. The consecrated blade upon my knees
Is Sato's ancient blade, still as it was,
Still razor-keen, still like a looking-glass
Unspotted by the centuries;
That flowering, silken, old embroidery, torn
From some court-lady's dress and round
The wooden scabbard bound and wound,
Can, tattered, still protect, faded adorn.

My Soul. Why should the imagination of a man
Long past his prime remember things that are
Emblematical of love and war?
Think of ancestral night that can,
If but imagination scorn the earth
And intellect its wandering
To this and that and t'other thing,
Deliver from the crime of death and birth.

My Self. Montashigi, third of his family, fashioned it
Five hundred years ago, about it lie
Flowers from I know not what embroidery —
Heart's purple — and all these I set
For emblems of the day against the tower
Emblematical of the night,
And claim as by a soldier's right
A charter to commit the crime once more.

My Soul. Such fullness in that quarter overflows
And falls into the basin of the mind
That man is stricken deaf and dumb and blind,

For intellect no longer knows
Is from the *Ought*, or *Knower* from the *Known* —
That is to say, ascends to Heaven;
Only the dead can be forgiven;
But when I think of that my tongue's a stone.

II

My Self. A living man is blind and drinks his drop.
What matter if the ditches are impure?
What matter if I live it all once more?
Endure that toil of growing up;
The ignominy of boyhood; the distress
Of boyhood changing into man;
The unfinished man and his pain
Brought face to face with his own clumsiness;

The finished man among his enemies? —
How in the name of Heaven can he escape
That defiling and disfigured shape
The mirror of malicious eyes
Casts upon his eyes until at last
He thinks that shape must be his shape?
And what's the good of an escape
If honour find him in the wintry blast?

I am content to live it all again
And yet again, if it be life to pitch
Into the frog-spawn of a blind man's ditch,
A blind man battering blind men;
Or into that most fecund ditch of all,
The folly that man does
Or must suffer, if he woos
A proud woman not kindred of his soul.

I am content to follow to its source
Every event in action or in thought;
Measure the lot; forgive myself the lot!
When such as I cast out remorse
So great a sweetness flows into the breast
We must laugh and we must sing,
We are blest by everything,
Everything we look upon is blest.

BLOOD AND THE MOON

I

BLESSED be this place,
More blessed still this tower;
A bloody, arrogant power
Rose out of the race
Uttering, mastering it,
Rose like these walls from these
Storm-beaten cottages —
In mockery I have set
A powerful emblem up,
And sing it rhyme upon rhyme
In mockery of a time
Half dead at the top.

II

Alexandria's was a beacon tower, and Babylon's
An image of the moving heavens, a log-book of the sun's
    journey and the moon's;
And Shelley had his towers, thought's crowned powers he
    called them once.

I declare this tower is my symbol; I declare
This winding, gyring, spiring treadmill of a stair is my an-
cestral stair;
That Goldsmith and the Dean, Berkeley and Burke have
travelled there.

Swift beating on his breast in sibylline frenzy blind
Because the heart in his blood-sodden breast had dragged him
down into mankind,
Goldsmith deliberately sipping at the honey-pot of his mind,

And haughtier-headed Burke that proved the State a tree,
That this unconquerable labyrinth of the birds, century after
century,
Cast but dead leaves to mathematical equality;

And God-appointed Berkeley that proved all things a dream,
That this pragmatical, preposterous pig of a world, its farrow
that so solid seem,
Must vanish on the instant if the mind but change its theme;

Saeva Indignatio and the labourer's hire,
The strength that gives our blood and state magnanimity of
its own desire;
Everything that is not God consumed with intellectual fire.

III

The purity of the unclouded moon
Has flung its arrowy shaft upon the floor.
Seven centuries have passed and it is pure,
The blood of innocence has left no stain.
There, on blood-saturated ground, have stood
Soldier, assassin, executioner,

Whether for daily pittance or in blind fear
Or out of abstract hatred, and shed blood,
But could not cast a single jet thereon.
Odour of blood on the ancestral stair!
And we that have shed none must gather there
And clamour in drunken frenzy for the moon.

IV

Upon the dusty, glittering windows cling,
And seem to cling upon the moonlit skies,
Tortoiseshell butterflies, peacock butterflies,
A couple of night-moths are on the wing.
Is every modern nation like the tower,
Half dead at the top? No matter what I said,
For wisdom is the property of the dead,
A something incompatible with life; and power,
Like everything that has the stain of blood,
A property of the living; but no stain
Can come upon the visage of the moon
When it has looked in glory from a cloud.

THE SEVEN SAGES

The First. My great-grandfather spoke to Edmund Burke
In Grattan's house.

The Second.   My great-grandfather shared
A pot-house bench with Oliver Goldsmith once.

The Third. My great-grandfather's father talked of music,
Drank tar-water with the Bishop of Cloyne.

The Fourth. But mine saw Stella once.

The Fifth.   Whence came our thought?

The Sixth. From four great minds that hated Whiggery.

The Fifth. Burke was a Whig.

The Sixth.   Whether they knew or not,
    Goldsmith and Burke, Swift and the Bishop of Cloyne
    All hated Whiggery; but what is Whiggery?
    A levelling, rancorous, rational sort of mind
    That never looked out of the eye of a saint
    Or out of drunkard's eye.

The Seventh.   All's Whiggery now,
    But we old men are massed against the world.

The First. American colonies, Ireland, France and India
    Harried, and Burke's great melody against it.

The Second. Oliver Goldsmith sang what he had seen,
    Roads full of beggars, cattle in the fields,
    But never saw the trefoil stained with blood,
    The avenging leaf those fields raised up against it.

The Fourth. The tomb of Swift wears it away.

The Third.   A voice
    Soft as the rustle of a reed from Cloyne
    That gathers volume; now a thunder-clap.

The Sixth. What schooling had these four?

The Seventh.   They walked the roads
    Mimicking what they heard, as children mimic;
    They understood that wisdom comes of beggary.

COOLE PARK, 1929

I MEDITATE upon a swallow's flight,
Upon an aged woman and her house,
A sycamore and lime-tree lost in night
Although that western cloud is luminous,
Great works constructed there in nature's spite
For scholars and for poets after us,
Thoughts long knitted into a single thought,
A dance-like glory that those walls begot.

There Hyde before he had beaten into prose
That noble blade the Muses buckled on,
There one that ruffled in a manly pose
For all his timid heart, there that slow man,
That meditative man, John Synge, and those
Impetuous men, Shawe-Taylor and Hugh Lane,
Found pride established in humility,
A scene well set and excellent company.

They came like swallows and like swallows went,
And yet a woman's powerful character
Could keep a swallow to its first intent;
And half a dozen in formation there,
That seemed to whirl upon a compass-point,
Found certainty upon the dreaming air,
The intellectual sweetness of those lines
That cut through time or cross it withershins.

Here, traveller, scholar, poet, take your stand
When all those rooms and passages are gone,

When nettles wave upon a shapeless mound
And saplings root among the broken stone,
And dedicate — eyes bent upon the ground,
Back turned upon the brightness of the sun
And all the sensuality of the shade —
A moment's memory to that laurelled head.

COOLE PARK AND BALLYLEE, 1931

UNDER my window-ledge the waters race,
Otters below and moor-hens on the top,
Run for a mile undimmed in Heaven's face
Then darkening through 'dark' Raftery's 'cellar' drop,
Run underground, rise in a rocky place
In Coole demesne, and there to finish up
Spread to a lake and drop into a hole.
What's water but the generated soul?

Upon the border of that lake's a wood
Now all dry sticks under a wintry sun,
And in a copse of beeches there I stood,
For Nature's pulled her tragic buskin on
And all the rant's a mirror of my mood:
At sudden thunder of the mounting swan
I turned about and looked where branches break
The glittering reaches of the flooded lake.

Another emblem there! That stormy white
But seems a concentration of the sky;
And, like the soul, it sails into the sight
And in the morning's gone, no man knows why;
And is so lovely that it sets to right
What knowledge or its lack had set awry,

So arrogantly pure, a child might think
It can be murdered with a spot of ink.

Sound of a stick upon the floor, a sound
From somebody that toils from chair to chair;
Beloved books that famous hands have bound,
Old marble heads, old pictures everywhere;
Great rooms where travelled men and children found
Content or joy; a last inheritor
Where none has reigned that lacked a name and fame
Or out of folly into folly came.

A spot whereon the founders lived and died
Seemed once more dear than life; ancestral trees,
Or gardens rich in memory glorified
Marriages, alliances and families,
And every bride's ambition satisfied.
Where fashion or mere fantasy decrees
We shift about — all that great glory spent —
Like some poor Arab tribesman and his tent.

We were the last romantics — chose for theme
Traditional sanctity and loveliness;
Whatever's written in what poets name
The book of the people; whatever most can bless
The mind of man or elevate a rhyme;
But all is changed, that high horse riderless,
Though mounted in that saddle Homer rode
Where the swan drifts upon a darkening flood.

SWIFT'S EPITAPH

SWIFT has sailed into his rest;
Savage indignation there
Cannot lacerate his breast.
Imitate him if you dare,
World-besotted traveller; he
Served human liberty.

AT ALGECIRAS — A MEDITATION UPON DEATH

THE heron-billed pale cattle-birds
That feed on some foul parasite
Of the Moroccan flocks and herds
Cross the narrow Straits to light
In the rich midnight of the garden trees
Till the dawn break upon those mingled seas.

Often at evening when a boy
Would I carry to a friend —
Hoping more substantial joy
Did an older mind commend —
Not such as are in Newton's metaphor,
But actual shells of Rosses' level shore.

Greater glory in the sun,
An evening chill upon the air,
Bid imagination run
Much on the Great Questioner;
What He can question, what if questioned I
Can with a fitting confidence reply.

November 1928

THE CHOICE

THE intellect of man is forced to choose
Perfection of the life, or of the work,
And if it take the second must refuse
A heavenly mansion, raging in the dark.
When all that story's finished, what's the news?
In luck or out the toil has left its mark:
That old perplexity an empty purse,
Or the day's vanity, the night's remorse.

BYZANTIUM

THE unpurged images of day recede;
The Emperor's drunken soldiery are abed;
Night resonance recedes, night-walkers' song
After great cathedral gong;
A starlit or a moonlit dome disdains
All that man is,
All mere complexities,
The fury and the mire of human veins.

Before me floats an image, man or shade,
Shade more than man, more image than a shade;
For Hades' bobbin bound in mummy-cloth
May unwind the winding path;
A mouth that has no moisture and no breath
Breathless mouths may summon;
I hail the superhuman;
I call it death-in-life and life-in-death.

Miracle, bird or golden handiwork,
More miracle than bird or handiwork,
Planted on the star-lit golden bough,
Can like the cocks of Hades crow,
Or, by the moon embittered, scorn aloud
In glory of changeless metal
Common bird or petal
And all complexities of mire or blood.

At midnight on the Emperor's pavement flit
Flames that no faggot feeds, nor steel has lit,
Nor storm disturbs, flames begotten of flame,
Where blood-begotten spirits come
And all complexities of fury leave,
Dying into a dance,
An agony of trance,
An agony of flame that cannot singe a sleeve.

Astraddle on the dolphin's mire and blood,
Spirit after spirit! The smithies break the flood,
The golden smithies of the Emperor!
Marbles of the dancing floor
Break bitter furies of complexity,
Those images that yet
Fresh images beget,
That dolphin-torn, that gong-tormented sea.

1930

THE MOTHER OF GOD

THE threefold terror of love; a fallen flare
Through the hollow of an ear;
Wings beating about the room;
The terror of all terrors that I bore
The Heavens in my womb.

Had I not found content among the shows
Every common woman knows,
Chimney corner, garden walk,
Or rocky cistern where we tread the clothes
And gather all the talk?

What is this flesh I purchased with my pains,
This fallen star my milk sustains,
This love that makes my heart's blood stop
Or strikes a sudden chill into my bones
And bids my hair stand up?

VACILLATION

I

BETWEEN extremities
Man runs his course;
A brand, or flaming breath,
Comes to destroy
All those antinomies
Of day and night;
The body calls it death,
The heart remorse.
But if these be right
What is joy?

II

A tree there is that from its topmost bough
Is half all glittering flame and half all green
Abounding foliage moistened with the dew;
And half is half and yet is all the scene;
And half and half consume what they renew,
And he that Attis' image hangs between
That staring fury and the blind lush leaf
May know not what he knows, but knows not grief.

III

Get all the gold and silver that you can,
Satisfy ambition, animate
The trivial days and ram them with the sun,
And yet upon these maxims meditate:
All women dote upon an idle man
Although their children need a rich estate;
No man has ever lived that had enough
Of children's gratitude or woman's love.

No longer in Lethean foliage caught
Begin the preparation for your death
And from the fortieth winter by that thought
Test every work of intellect or faith,
And everything that your own hands have wrought,
And call those works extravagance of breath
That are not suited for such men as come
Proud, open-eyed and laughing to the tomb.

IV

My fiftieth year had come and gone,
I sat, a solitary man,

In a crowded London shop,
An open book and empty cup
On the marble table-top.

While on the shop and street I gazed
My body of a sudden blazed;
And twenty minutes more or less
It seemed, so great my happiness,
That I was blessèd and could bless.

V

Although the summer sunlight gild
Cloudy leafage of the sky,
Or wintry moonlight sink the field
In storm-scattered intricacy,
I cannot look thereon,
Responsibility so weighs me down.

Things said or done long years ago,
Or things I did not do or say
But thought that I might say or do,
Weigh me down, and not a day
But something is recalled,
My conscience or my vanity appalled.

VI

A rivery field spread out below,
An odour of the new-mown hay
In his nostrils, the great lord of Chou
Cried, casting off the mountain snow,
'Let all things pass away.'

Wheels by milk-white asses drawn
Where Babylon or Nineveh
Rose; some conqueror drew rein
And cried to battle-weary men,
'Let all things pass away.'

From man's blood-sodden heart are sprung
Those branches of the night and day
Where the gaudy moon is hung.
What's the meaning of all song?
'Let all things pass away.'

VII

The Soul. Seek out reality, leave things that seem.

The Heart. What, be a singer born and lack a theme?

The Soul. Isaiah's coal, what more can man desire?

The Heart. Struck dumb in the simplicity of fire!

The Soul. Look on that fire, salvation walks within.

The Heart. What theme had Homer but original sin?

VIII

Must we part, Von Hügel, though much alike, for we
Accept the miracles of the saints and honour sanctity?
The body of Saint Teresa lies undecayed in tomb,
Bathed in miraculous oil, sweet odours from it come,
Healing from its lettered slab. Those self-same hands perchance
Eternalised the body of a modern saint that once

Had scooped out Pharaoh's mummy. I — though heart
   might find relief
Did I become a Christian man and choose for my belief
What seems most welcome in the tomb — play a predestined
   part.
Homer is my example and his unchristened heart.
The lion and the honeycomb, what has Scripture said?
So get you gone, Von Hügel, though with blessings on your
   head.

   1932

REMORSE FOR INTEMPERATE SPEECH

I RANTED to the knave and fool,
But outgrew that school,
Would transform the part,
Fit audience found, but cannot rule
My fanatic[1] heart.

I sought my betters: though in each
Fine manners, liberal speech,
Turn hatred into sport,
Nothing said or done can reach
My fanatic heart.

Out of Ireland have we come.
Great hatred, little room,
Maimed us at the start.
I carry from my mother's womb
A fanatic heart.

   August 28, 1931

[1] I pronounce 'fanatic' in what is, I suppose, the older and more
Irish way, so that the last line of each stanza contains but two beats.

V

CRAZY JANE ON GOD

THAT lover of a night
Came when he would,
Went in the dawning light
Whether I would or no;
Men come, men go;
All things remain in God.

Banners choke the sky;
Men-at-arms tread;
Armoured horses neigh
Where the great battle was
In the narrow pass:
All things remain in God.

Before their eyes a house
That from childhood stood
Uninhabited, ruinous,
Suddenly lit up
From door to top:
All things remain in God.

I had wild Jack for a lover;
Though like a road
That men pass over
My body makes no moan
But sings on:
All things remain in God.

VI

CRAZY JANE TALKS WITH THE BISHOP

I MET the Bishop on the road
And much said he and I.
'Those breasts are flat and fallen now,
Those veins must soon be dry;
Live in a heavenly mansion,
Not in some foul sty.'

'Fast and foul are near of kin,
And fair needs foul,' I cried.
'My friends are gone, but that's a truth
Nor grave nor bed denied,
Learned in bodily lowliness
And in the heart's pride.

'A woman can be proud and stiff
When on love intent;
But Love has pitched his mansion in
The place of excrement;
For nothing can be sole or whole
That has not been rent.'

VII

CRAZY JANE GROWN OLD LOOKS AT THE DANCERS

I FOUND that ivory image there
Dancing with her chosen youth,
But when he wound her coal-black hair

As though to strangle her, no scream
Or bodily movement did I dare,
Eyes under eyelids did so gleam;
Love is like the lion's tooth.

When she, and though some said she played
I said that she had danced heart's truth,
Drew a knife to strike him dead,
I could but leave him to his fate;
For no matter what is said
They had all that had their hate;
Love is like the lion's tooth.

Did he die or did she die?
Seemed to die or died they both?
God be with the times when I
Cared not a thraneen for what chanced
So that I had the limbs to try
Such a dance as there was danced —
Love is like the lion's tooth.

XIV

HIS BARGAIN

WHO talks of Plato's spindle;
What set it whirling round?
Eternity may dwindle,
Time is unwound,
Dan and Jerry Lout
Change their loves about.

However they may take it,
Before the thread began
I made, and may not break it
When the last thread has run,
A bargain with that hair
And all the windings there.

XVI

LULLABY

BELOVED, may your sleep be sound
That have found it where you fed.
What were all the world's alarms
To mighty Paris when he found
Sleep upon a golden bed
That first dawn in Helen's arms?

Sleep, beloved, such a sleep
As did that wild Tristram know
When, the potion's work being done,
Roe could run or doe could leap
Under oak and beechen bough,
Roe could leap or doe could run;

Such a sleep and sound as fell
Upon Eurotas' grassy bank
When the holy bird, that there
Accomplished his predestined will,
From the limbs of Leda sank
But not from her protecting care.

XVII
AFTER LONG SILENCE

SPEECH after long silence; it is right,
All other lovers being estranged or dead,
Unfriendly lamplight hid under its shade,
The curtains drawn upon unfriendly night,
That we descant and yet again descant
Upon the supreme theme of Art and Song:
Bodily decrepitude is wisdom; young
We loved each other and were ignorant.

XVIII
MAD AS THE MIST AND SNOW

BOLT and bar the shutter,
For the foul winds blow:
Our minds are at their best this night,
And I seem to know
That everything outside us is
Mad as the mist and snow.

Horace there by Homer stands,
Plato stands below,
And here is Tully's open page.
How many years ago
Were you and I unlettered lads
Mad as the mist and snow?

You ask what makes me sigh, old friend,
What makes me shudder so?
I shudder and I sigh to think
That even Cicero
And many-minded Homer were
Mad as the mist and snow.

XX

'I AM OF IRELAND'

'*I AM of Ireland,*
And the Holy Land of Ireland,
And time runs on,' cried she:
'*Come out of charity,*
Come dance with me in Ireland.'

One man, one man alone
In that outlandish gear,
One solitary man
Of all that rambled there
Had turned his stately head.
'That is a long way off,
And time runs on,' he said,
'And the night grows rough.'

'*I am of Ireland,*
And the Holy Land of Ireland,
And time runs on,' cried she.
'*Come out of charity*
And dance with me in Ireland.'

'The fiddlers are all thumbs,
Or the fiddle-string accursed,
The drums and the kettledrums
And the trumpets all are burst,
And the trombone,' cried he,
'The trumpet and trombone,'
And cocked a malicious eye,
'But time runs on, runs on.'

'I am of Ireland,
And the Holy Land of Ireland,
And time runs on,' cried she.
'Come out of charity
And dance with me in Ireland.'

XXIV

OLD TOM AGAIN

THINGS out of perfection sail,
And all their swelling canvas wear,
Nor shall the self-begotten fail
Though fantastic men suppose
Building-yard and stormy shore,
Winding-sheet and swaddling-clothes.

XXV

THE DELPHIC ORACLE UPON PLOTINUS

BEHOLD that great Plotinus swim,
Buffeted by such seas;
Bland Rhadamanthus beckons him,
But the Golden Race looks dim,
Salt blood blocks his eyes.

Scattered on the level grass
Or winding through the grove
Plato there and Minos pass,
There stately Pythagoras
And all the choir of Love.

August 19, 1931

From *A WOMAN YOUNG AND OLD*

FATHER AND CHILD

SHE hears me strike the board and say
That she is under ban
Of all good men and women,
Being mentioned with a man
That has the worst of all bad names;
And thereupon replies
That his hair is beautiful,
Cold as the March wind his eyes.

II

BEFORE THE WORLD WAS MADE

IF I make the lashes dark
And the eyes more bright
And the lips more scarlet,
Or ask if all be right
From mirror after mirror,
No vanity's displayed:
I'm looking for the face I had
Before the world was made.

What if I look upon a man
As though on my beloved,
And my blood be cold the while
And my heart unmoved?

Why should he think me cruel
Or that he is betrayed?
I'd have him love the thing that was
Before the world was made.

IV

HER TRIUMPH

I DID the dragon's will until you came
Because I had fancied love a casual
Improvisation, or a settled game
That followed if I let the kerchief fall:
Those deeds were best that gave the minute wings
And heavenly music if they gave it wit;
And then you stood among the dragon-rings.
I mocked, being crazy, but you mastered it
And broke the chain and set my ankles free,
Saint George or else a pagan Perseus;
And now we stare astonished at the sea,
And a miraculous strange bird shrieks at us.

V

CONSOLATION

O BUT there is wisdom
In what the sages said;
But stretch that body for a while
And lay down that head
Till I have told the sages
Where man is comforted.

How could passion run so deep
Had I never thought
That the crime of being born
Blackens all our lot?
But where the crime's committed
The crime can be forgot.

VI

CHOSEN

THE lot of love is chosen. I learnt that much
Struggling for an image on the track
Of the whirling Zodiac.
Scarce did he my body touch,
Scarce sank he from the west
Or found a subterranean rest
On the maternal midnight of my breast
Before I had marked him on his northern way,
And seemed to stand although in bed I lay.

I struggled with the horror of daybreak,
I chose it for my lot! If questioned on
My utmost pleasure with a man
By some new-married bride, I take
That stillness for a theme
Where his heart my heart did seem
And both adrift on the miraculous stream
Where — wrote a learned astrologer —
The Zodiac is changed into a sphere.

VII

PARTING

He. Dear, I must be gone
    While night shuts the eyes
    Of the household spies;
    That song announces dawn.

  She. No, night's bird and love's
    Bids all true lovers rest,
    While his loud song reproves
    The murderous stealth of day.

  He. Daylight already flies
    From mountain crest to crest.

  She. That light is from the moon.

  He. That bird . . .

  She.   Let him sing on,
    I offer to love's play
    My dark declivities.

VIII

HER VISION IN THE WOOD

DRY timber under that rich foliage,
At wine-dark midnight in the sacred wood,
Too old for a man's love I stood in rage
Imagining men. Imagining that I could
A greater with a lesser pang assuage

Or but to find if withered vein ran blood,
I tore my body that its wine might cover
Whatever could recall the lip of lover.

And after that I held my fingers up,
Stared at the wine-dark nail, or dark that ran
Down every withered finger from the top;
But the dark changed to red, and torches shone,
And deafening music shook the leaves; a troop
Shouldered a litter with a wounded man,
Or smote upon the string and to the sound
Sang of the beast that gave the fatal wound.

All stately women moving to a song
With loosened hair or foreheads grief-distraught,
It seemed a Quattrocento painter's throng,
A thoughtless image of Mantegna's thought —
Why should they think that are for ever young?
Till suddenly in grief's contagion caught,
I stared upon his blood-bedabbled breast
And sang my malediction with the rest.

That thing all blood and mire, that beast-torn wreck,
Half turned and fixed a glazing eye on mine,
And, though love's bitter-sweet had all come back,
Those bodies from a picture or a coin
Nor saw my body fall nor heard it shriek,
Nor knew, drunken with singing as with wine,
That they had brought no fabulous symbol there
But my heart's victim and its torturer.

IX

A LAST CONFESSION

WHAT lively lad most pleasured me
Of all that with me lay?
I answer that I gave my soul
And loved in misery,
But had great pleasure with a lad
That I loved bodily.

Flinging from his arms I laughed
To think his passion such
He fancied that I gave a soul
Did but our bodies touch,
And laughed upon his breast to think
Beast gave beast as much.

I gave what other women gave
That stepped out of their clothes,
But when this soul, its body off,
Naked to naked goes,
He it has found shall find therein
What none other knows,

And give his own and take his own
And rule in his own right;
And though it loved in misery
Close and cling so tight,
There's not a bird of day that dare
Extinguish that delight.

XI

FROM THE 'ANTIGONE'

OVERCOME — O bitter sweetness,
Inhabitant of the soft cheek of a girl —
The rich man and his affairs,
The fat flocks and the fields' fatness,
Mariners, rough harvesters;
Overcome Gods upon Parnassus;

Overcome the Empyrean; hurl
Heaven and Earth out of their places,
That in the same calamity
Brother and brother, friend and friend,
Family and family,
City and city may contend,
By that great glory driven wild.

Pray I will and sing I must,
And yet I weep — Oedipus' child
Descends into the loveless dust.

From *A FULL MOON IN MARCH*

PARNELL'S FUNERAL

I

UNDER the Great Comedian's tomb the crowd,
A bundle of tempestuous cloud is blown
About the sky; where that is clear of cloud
Brightness remains; a brighter star shoots down;
What shudders run through all that animal blood?
What is this sacrifice? Can someone there
Recall the Cretan barb that pierced a star?

Rich foliage that the starlight glittered through,
A frenzied crowd, and where the branches sprang
A beautiful seated boy; a sacred bow;
A woman, and an arrow on a string;
A pierced boy, image of a star laid low.
That woman, the Great Mother imaging,
Cut out his heart. Some master of design
Stamped boy and tree upon Sicilian coin.

An age is the reversal of an age:
When strangers murdered Emmet, Fitzgerald, Tone,
We lived like men that watch a painted stage.
What matter for the scene, the scene once gone:
It had not touched our lives. But popular rage,
Hysterica passio dragged this quarry down.
None shared our guilt; nor did we play a part
Upon a painted stage when we devoured his heart.

Come, fix upon me that accusing eye.
I thirst for accusation. All that was sung,
All that was said in Ireland is a lie
Bred out of the contagion of the throng,
Saving the rhyme rats hear before they die.
Leave nothing but the nothings that belong
To this bare soul, let all men judge that can
Whether it be an animal or a man.

II

The rest I pass, one sentence I unsay.
Had de Valéra eaten Parnell's heart
No loose-lipped demagogue had won the day,
No civil rancour torn the land apart.

Had Cosgrave eaten Parnell's heart, the land's
Imagination had been satisfied,
Or lacking that, government in such hands,
O'Higgins its sole statesman had not died.

Had even O'Duffy — but I name no more —
Their school a crowd, his master solitude;
Through Jonathan Swift's dark grove he passed, and there
Plucked bitter wisdom that enriched his blood.

A PRAYER FOR OLD AGE

God guard me from those thoughts men think
In the mind alone;
He that sings a lasting song
Thinks in a marrow-bone;

From all that makes a wise old man
That can be praised of all;
O what am I that I should not seem
For the song's sake a fool?

I pray — for fashion's word is out
And prayer comes round again —
That I may seem, though I die old,
A foolish, passionate man.

SUPERNATURAL SONGS

I

Ribh at the Tomb of Baile and Aillinn

BECAUSE you have found me in the pitch-dark night
With open book you ask me what I do.
Mark and digest my tale, carry it afar
To those that never saw this tonsured head
Nor heard this voice that ninety years have cracked.
Of Baile and Aillinn you need not speak,
All know their tale, all know what leaf and twig,
What juncture of the apple and the yew,
Surmount their bones; but speak what none have heard.

The miracle that gave them such a death
Transfigured to pure substance what had once
Been bone and sinew; when such bodies join
There is no touching here, nor touching there,
Nor straining joy, but whole is joined to whole;
For the intercourse of angels is a light
Where for its moment both seem lost, consumed.

Here in the pitch-dark atmosphere above
The trembling of the apple and the yew,
Here on the anniversary of their death,
The anniversary of their first embrace,
Those lovers, purified by tragedy,
Hurry into each other's arms; these eyes,
By water, herb and solitary prayer
Made aquiline, are open to that light.
Though somewhat broken by the leaves, that light
Lies in a circle on the grass; therein
I turn the pages of my holy book.

IV

There

THERE all the barrel-hoops are knit,
There all the serpent-tails are bit,
There all the gyres converge in one,
There all the planets drop in the Sun.

V

Ribh considers Christian Love insufficient

Why should I seek for love or study it?
It is of God and passes human wit.
I study hatred with great diligence,
For that's a passion in my own control,
A sort of besom that can clear the soul
Of everything that is not mind or sense.

Why do I hate man, woman or event?
That is a light my jealous soul has sent.

From terror and deception freed it can
Discover impurities, can show at last
How soul may walk when all such things are past,
How soul could walk before such things began.

Then my delivered soul herself shall learn
A darker knowledge and in hatred turn
From every thought of God mankind has had.
Thought is a garment and the soul's a bride
That cannot in that trash and tinsel hide:
Hatred of God may bring the soul to God.

At stroke of midnight soul cannot endure
A bodily or mental furniture.
What can she take until her Master give!
Where can she look until He make the show!
What can she know until He bid her know!
How can she live till in her blood He live!

VIII

Whence had they come?

Eternity is passion, girl or boy
Cry at the onset of their sexual joy
'For ever and for ever'; then awake
Ignorant what Dramatis Personae spake;
A passion-driven exultant man sings out
Sentences that he has never thought;
The Flagellant lashes those submissive loins
Ignorant what that dramatist enjoins,
What master made the lash. Whence had they come,
The hand and lash that beat down frigid Rome?
What sacred drama through her body heaved
When world-transforming Charlemagne was conceived?

IX

The Four Ages of Man

He with body waged a fight,
But body won; it walks upright.

Then he struggled with the heart;
Innocence and peace depart.

Then he struggled with the mind;
His proud heart he left behind.

Now his wars on God begin;
At stroke of midnight God shall win.

XII

Meru

Civilisation is hooped together, brought
Under a rule, under the semblance of peace
By manifold illusion; but man's life is thought,
And he, despite his terror, cannot cease
Ravening through century after century,
Ravening, raging, and uprooting that he may come
Into the desolation of reality:
Egypt and Greece, goodbye, and good-bye, Rome!
Hermits upon Mount Meru or Everest,
Caverned in night under the drifted snow,
Or where that snow and winter's dreadful blast
Beat down upon their naked bodies, know
That day brings round the night, that before dawn
His glory and his monuments are gone.

From *LAST POEMS*

THE GYRES

THE Gyres! the gyres! Old Rocky Face, look forth;
Things thought too long can be no longer thought,
For beauty dies of beauty, worth of worth,
And ancient lineaments are blotted out.
Irrational streams of blood are staining earth;
Empedocles has thrown all things about;
Hector is dead and there's a light in Troy;
We that look on but laugh in tragic joy.

What matter though numb nightmare ride on top,
And blood and mire the sensitive body stain?
What matter? Heave no sigh, let no tear drop,
A greater, a more gracious time has gone;
For painted forms or boxes of make-up
In ancient tombs I sighed, but not again;
What matter? Out of cavern comes a voice,
And all it knows is that one word 'Rejoice!'

Conduct and work grow coarse, and coarse the soul,
What matter? Those that Rocky Face holds dear,
Lovers of horses and of women, shall,
From marble of a broken sepulchre,
Or dark betwixt the polecat and the owl,
Or any rich, dark nothing disinter
The workman, noble and saint, and all things run
On that unfashionable gyre again.

LAPIS LAZULI

I HAVE heard that hysterical women say
They are sick of the palette and fiddle-bow,
Of poets that are always gay,
For everybody knows or else should know
That if nothing drastic is done
Aeroplane and Zeppelin will come out,
Pitch like King Billy bomb-balls in
Until the town lie beaten flat.

All perform their tragic play,
There struts Hamlet, there is Lear,
That's Ophelia, that Cordelia;
Yet they, should the last scene be there,
The great stage curtain about to drop,
If worthy their prominent part in the play,
Do not break up their lines to weep.
They know that Hamlet and Lear are gay;
Gaiety transfiguring all that dread.
All men have aimed at, found and lost;
Black out; Heaven blazing into the head:
Tragedy wrought to its uttermost.
Though Hamlet rambles and Lear rages,
And all the drop-scenes drop at once
Upon a hundred thousand stages,
It cannot grow by an inch or an ounce.

On their own feet they came, or on shipboard,
Camel-back, horse-back, ass-back, mule-back,
Old civilisations put to the sword.
Then they and their wisdom went to rack:

No handiwork of Callimachus,
Who handled marble as if it were bronze,
Made draperies that seemed to rise
When sea-wind swept the corner, stands:
His long lamp-chimney shaped like the stem
Of a slender palm, stood but a day;
All things fall and are built again,
And those that build them again are gay.

Two Chinamen, behind them a third,
Are carved in lapis lazuli,
Over them flies a long-legged bird,
A symbol of longevity;
The third, doubtless a serving-man,
Carries a musical instrument.

Every discoloration of the stone,
Every accidental crack or dent,
Seems a water-course or an avalanche,
Or lofty slope where it still snows
Though doubtless plum or cherry-branch
Sweetens the little half-way house
Those Chinamen climb towards, and I
Delight to imagine them seated there;
There, on the mountain and the sky,
On all the tragic scene they stare.
One asks for mournful melodies;
Accomplished fingers begin to play.
Their eyes mid many wrinkles, their eyes,
Their ancient, glittering eyes, are gay.

AN ACRE OF GRASS

PICTURE and book remain,
An acre of green grass
For air and exercise,
Now strength of body goes;
Midnight, an old house
Where nothing stirs but a mouse.

My temptation is quiet.
Here at life's end
Neither loose imagination,
Nor the mill of the mind
Consuming its rag and bone,
Can make the truth known.

Grant me an old man's frenzy,
Myself must I remake
Till I am Timon and Lear
Or that William Blake
Who beat upon the wall
Till Truth obeyed his call;

A mind Michael Angelo knew
That can pierce the clouds,
Or inspired by frenzy
Shake the dead in their shrouds;
Forgotten else by mankind,
An old man's eagle mind.

WHAT THEN?

His chosen cómrades thought at school
He must grow a famous man;
He thought the same and lived by rule,
All his twenties crammed with toil;
'*What then?*' *sang Plato's ghost.* '*What then?*'

Everything he wrote was read,
After certain years he won
Sufficient money for his need,
Friends that have been friends indeed;
'*What then?*' *sang Plato's ghost.* '*What then?*'

All his happier dreams came true —
A small old house, wife, daughter, son,
Grounds where plum and cabbage grew,
Poets and Wits about him drew;
'*What then?*' *sang Plato's ghost.* '*What then?*'

'The work is done,' grown old he thought,
'According to my boyish plan;
Let the fools rage, I swerved in naught,
Something to perfection brought';
But louder sang that ghost, '*What then?*'

BEAUTIFUL LOFTY THINGS

Beautiful lofty things: O'Leary's noble head;
My father upon the Abbey stage, before him a raging crowd:
'This Land of Saints,' and then as the applause died out,

'Of plaster Saints'; his beautiful mischievous head thrown
    back.
Standish O'Grady supporting himself between the tables
Speaking to a drunken audience high nonsensical words;
Augusta Gregory seated at her great ormolu table,
Her eightieth winter approaching: 'Yesterday he threatened
    my life.
I told him that nightly from six to seven I sat at this table,
The blinds drawn up'; Maud Gonne at Howth station waiting
    a train,
Pallas Athene in that straight back and arrogant head:
All the Olympians; a thing never known again.

THE CURSE OF CROMWELL

You ask what I have found, and far and wide I go:
Nothing but Cromwell's house and Cromwell's murderous
    crew,
The lovers and the dancers are beaten into the clay,
And the tall men and the swordsmen and the horsemen, where
    are they?
And there is an old beggar wandering in his pride —
His fathers served their fathers before Christ was crucified.

                O what of that, O what of that,
                What is there left to say?

All neighbourly content and easy talk are gone,
But there's no good complaining, for money's rant is on.
He that's mounting up must on his neighbour mount,
And we and all the Muses are things of no account.

They have schooling of their own, but I pass their schooling
   by,
What can they know that we know that know the time to
   die?

> *O what of that, O what of that,*
> *What is there left to say?*

But there's another knowledge that my heart destroys,
As the fox in the old fable destroyed the Spartan boy's,
Because it proves that things both can and cannot be;
That the swordsmen and the ladies can still keep company,
Can pay the poet for a verse and hear the fiddle sound,
That I am still their servant though all are underground.

> *O what of that, O what of that,*
> *What is there left to say?*

I came on a great house in the middle of the night,
Its open lighted doorway and its windows all alight,
And all my friends were there and made me welcome too;
But I woke in an old ruin that the winds howled through;
And when I pay attention I must out and walk
Among the dogs and horses that understand my talk.

> *O what of that, O what of that,*
> *What is there left to say?*

COME GATHER ROUND ME, PARNELLITES

> COME gather round me, Parnellites,
> And praise our chosen man;
> Stand upright on your legs awhile,
> Stand upright while you can,

For soon we lie where he is laid,
And he is underground;
Come fill up all those glasses
And pass the bottle round.

And here's a cogent reason,
And I have many more,
He fought the might of England
And saved the Irish poor,
Whatever good a farmer's got
He brought it all to pass;
And here's another reason,
That Parnell loved a lass.

And here's a final reason,
He was of such a kind
Every man that sings a song
Keeps Parnell in his mind.
For Parnell was a proud man,
No prouder trod the ground,
And a proud man's a lovely man,
So pass the bottle round.

The Bishops and the Party
That tragic story made,
A husband that had sold his wife
And after that betrayed;
But stories that live longest
Are sung above the glass,
And Parnell loved his country,
And Parnell loved his lass.

THE WILD OLD WICKED MAN

'BECAUSE I am mad about women
I am mad about the hills,'
Said that wild old wicked man
Who travels where God wills.
'Not to die on the straw at home,
Those hands to close these eyes,
That is all I ask, my dear,
From the old man in the skies.
                    Daybreak and a candle-end.

'Kind are all your words, my dear,
Do not the rest withhold.
Who can know the year, my dear,
When an old man's blood grows cold?
I have what no young man can have
Because he loves too much.
Words I have that can pierce the heart,
But what can he do but touch?'
                    Daybreak and a candle-end.

Then said she to that wild old man,
His stout stick under his hand,
'Love to give or to withhold
Is not at my command.
I gave it all to an older man:
That old man in the skies.
Hands that are busy with His beads
Can never close those eyes.'
                    Daybreak and a candle-end.

'Go your ways, O go your ways,
I choose another mark,
Girls down on the seashore
Who understand the dark;
Bawdy talk for the fishermen;
A dance for the fisher-lads;
When dark hangs upon the water
They turn down their beds.
                    Daybreak and a candle-end.

'A young man in the dark am I,
But a wild old man in the light,
That can make a cat laugh, or
Can touch by mother wit
Things hid in their marrow-bones
From time long passed away,
Hid from all those warty lads
That by their bodies lay.
                    Daybreak and a candle-end.

'All men live in suffering,
I know as few can know,
Whether they take the upper road
Or stay content on the low,
Rower bent in his row-boat
Or weaver bent at his loom,
Horseman erect upon horseback
Or child hid in the womb.
                    Daybreak and a candle-end.

'That some stream of lightning
From the old man in the skies
Can burn out that suffering
No right-taught man denies.

But a coarse old man am I,
I choose the second-best,
I forget it all awhile
Upon a woman's breast.'

Daybreak and a candle-end.

THE GREAT DAY

HURRAH for revolution and more cannon-shot!
A beggar upon horseback lashes a beggar on foot.
Hurrah for revolution and cannon come again!
The beggars have changed places, but the lash goes on.

THE SPUR

You think it horrible that lust and rage
Should dance attention upon my old age;
They were not such a plague when I was young;
What else have I to spur me into song?

THE PILGRIM

I FASTED for some forty days on bread and buttermilk,
For passing round the bottle with girls in rags or silk,
In country shawl or Paris cloak, had put my wits astray,
And what's the good of women, for all that they can say
Is fol de rol de rolly O.

Round Lough Derg's holy island I went upon the stones,
I prayed at all the Stations upon my marrow-bones,
And there I found an old man, and though I prayed all day
And that old man beside me, nothing would he say
But fol de rol de rolly O.

All know that all the dead in the world about that place are
    stuck,
And that should mother seek her son she'd have but little luck
Because the fires of Purgatory have ate their shapes away;
I swear to God I questioned them, and all they had to say
Was fol de rol de rolly O.

A great black ragged bird appeared when I was in the boat;
Some twenty feet from tip to tip had it stretched rightly out,
With flopping and with flapping it made a great display,
But I never stopped to question, what could the boatman say
But fol de rol de rolly O.

Now I am in the public-house and lean upon the wall,
So come in rags or come in silk, in cloak or country shawl,
And come with learned lovers or with what men you may,
For I can put the whole lot down, and all I have to say
Is fol de rol de rolly O.

THE MUNICIPAL GALLERY REVISITED

I

AROUND me the images of thirty years:
An ambush; pilgrims at the water-side;
Casement upon trial, half hidden by the bars,
Guarded; Griffith staring in hysterical pride;

Kevin O'Higgins' countenance that wears
A gentle questioning look that cannot hide
A soul incapable of remorse or rest;
A revolutionary soldier kneeling to be blessed;

II

An Abbot or Archbishop with an upraised hand
Blessing the Tricolour. 'This is not,' I say,
'The dead Ireland of my youth, but an Ireland
The poets have imagined, terrible and gay.'
Before a woman's portrait suddenly I stand,
Beautiful and gentle in her Venetian way.
I met her all but fifty years ago
For twenty minutes in some studio.

III

Heart-smitten with emotion I sink down,
My heart recovering with covered eyes;
Wherever I had looked I had looked upon
My permanent or impermanent images:
Augusta Gregory's son; her sister's son,
Hugh Lane, 'onlie begetter' of all these;
Hazel Lavery living and dying, that tale
As though some ballad-singer had sung it all;

IV

Mancini's portrait of Augusta Gregory,
'Greatest since Rembrandt,' according to John Synge;
A great ebullient portrait certainly;
But where is the brush that could show anything
Of all that pride and that humility?

And I am in despair that time may bring
Approved patterns of women or of men
But not that selfsame excellence again.

V

My mediaeval knees lack health until they bend,
But in that woman, in that household where
Honour had lived so long, all lacking found.
Childless I thought, 'My children may find here
Deep-rooted things,' but never foresaw its end,
And now that end has come I have not wept;
No fox can foul the lair the badger swept —

VI

(An image out of Spenser and the common tongue).
John Synge, I and Augusta Gregory, thought
All that we did, all that we said or sang
Must come from contact with the soil, from that
Contact everything Antaeus-like grew strong.
We three alone in modern times had brought
Everything down to that sole test again,
Dream of the noble and the beggar-man.

VII

And here's John Synge himself, that rooted man,
'Forgetting human words,' a grave deep face.
You that would judge me, do not judge alone
This book or that, come to this hallowed place
Where my friends' portraits hang and look thereon;
Ireland's history in their lineaments trace;
Think where man's glory most begins and ends,
And say my glory was I had such friends.

ARE YOU CONTENT?

I CALL on those that call me son,
Grandson, or great-grandson,
On uncles, aunts, great-uncles or great-aunts,
To judge what I have done.
Have I, that put it into words,
Spoilt what old loins have sent?
Eyes spiritualised by death can judge,
I cannot, but I am not content.

He that in Sligo at Drumcliff
Set up the old stone Cross,
That red-headed rector in County Down,
A good man on a horse,
Sandymount Corbets, that notable man
Old William Pollexfen,
The smuggler Middleton, Butlers far back,
Half legendary men.

Infirm and aged I might stay
In some good company,
I who have always hated work,
Smiling at the sea,
Or demonstrate in my own life
What Robert Browning meant
By an old hunter talking with Gods;
But I am not content.

THE STATUES

PYTHAGORAS planned it. Why did the people stare?
His numbers, though they moved or seemed to move
In marble or in bronze, lacked character.
But boys and girls, pale from the imagined love
Of solitary beds, knew what they were,
That passion could bring character enough,
And pressed at midnight in some public place
Live lips upon a plummet-measured face.

No! Greater than Pythagoras, for the men
That with a mallet or a chisel modelled these
Calculations that look but casual flesh, put down
All Asiatic vague immensities,
And not the banks of oars that swam upon
The many-headed foam at Salamis.
Europe put off that foam when Phidias
Gave women dreams and dreams their looking-glass.

One image crossed the many-headed, sat
Under the tropic shade, grew round and slow,
No Hamlet thin from eating flies, a fat
Dreamer of the Middle Ages. Empty eyeballs knew
That knowledge increases unreality, that
Mirror on mirror mirrored is all the show.
When gong and conch declare the hour to bless
Grimalkin crawls to Buddha's emptiness.

When Pearse summoned Cuchulain to his side,
What stalked through the Post Office? What intellect,
What calculation, number, measurement, replied?

We Irish, born into that ancient sect
But thrown upon this filthy modern tide
And by its formless spawning fury wrecked,
Climb to our proper dark, that we may trace
The lineaments of a plummet-measured face.

April 9, 1938

NEWS FOR THE DELPHIC ORACLE

I

THERE all the golden codgers lay,
There the silver dew,
And the great water sighed for love,
And the wind sighed too.
Man-picker Niamh leant and sighed
By Oisin on the grass;
There sighed amid his choir of love
Tall Pythagoras.
Plotinus came and looked about,
The salt-flakes on his breast,
And having stretched and yawned awhile
Lay sighing like the rest.

II

Straddling each a dolphin's back
And steadied by a fin,
Those Innocents re-live their death,
Their wounds open again.
The ecstatic waters laugh because
Their cries are sweet and strange,
Through their ancestral patterns dance,

And the brute dolphins plunge
Until, in some cliff-sheltered bay
Where wades the choir of love
Proffering its sacred laurel crowns,
They pitch their burdens off.

III

Slim adolescence that a nymph has stripped,
Peleus on Thetis stares.
Her limbs are delicate as an eyelid,
Love has blinded him with tears;
But Thetis' belly listens.
Down the mountain walls
From where Pan's cavern is
Intolerable music falls.
Foul goat-head, brutal arm appear,
Belly, shoulder, bum,
Flash fishlike; nymphs and satyrs
Copulate in the foam.

LONG-LEGGED FLY

THAT civilisation may not sink,
Its great battle lost,
Quiet the dog, tether the pony
To a distant post;
Our master Caesar is in the tent
Where the maps are spread,
His eyes fixed upon nothing,
A hand under his head.
Like a long-legged fly upon the stream
His mind moves upon silence.

That the topless towers be burnt
And men recall that face,
Move most gently if move you must
In this lonely place.
She thinks, part woman, three parts a child,
That nobody looks; her feet
Practise a tinker shuffle
Picked up on a street.
Like a long-legged fly upon the stream
Her mind moves upon silence.

That girls at puberty may find
The first Adam in their thought,
Shut the door of the Pope's chapel,
Keep those children out.
There on that scaffolding reclines
Michael Angelo.
With no more sound than the mice make
His hand moves to and fro.
Like a long-legged fly upon the stream
His mind moves upon silence.

A BRONZE HEAD

HERE at right of the entrance this bronze head,
Human, superhuman, a bird's round eye,
Everything else withered and mummy-dead.
What great tomb-haunter sweeps the distant sky
(Something may linger there though all else die;)
And finds there nothing to make its terror less
Hysterica passio of its own emptiness?

No dark tomb-haunter once; her form all full
As though with magnanimity of light,
Yet a most gentle woman; who can tell
Which of her forms has shown her substance right?
Or maybe substance can be composite,
Profound McTaggart thought so, and in a breath
A mouthful held the extreme of life and death.

But even at the starting-post, all sleek and new,
I saw the wildness in her and I thought
A vision of terror that it must live through
Had shattered her soul. Propinquity had brought
Imagination to that pitch where it casts out
All that is not itself: I had grown wild
And wandered murmuring everywhere, 'My child, my
      child!'

Or else I thought her supernatural;
As though a sterner eye looked through her eye
On this foul world in its decline and fall;
On gangling stocks grown great, great stocks run dry,
Ancestral pearls all pitched into a sty,
Heroic reverie mocked by clown and knave,
And wondered what was left for massacre to save.

HIGH TALK

PROCESSIONS that lack high stilts have nothing that catches the
      eye.
What if my great-granddad had a pair that were twenty foot
      high,
And mine were but fifteen foot, no modern stalks upon
      higher,

Some rogue of the world stole them to patch up a fence or a
     fire.
Because piebald ponies, led bears, caged lions, make but poor
     shows,
Because children demand Daddy-long-legs upon his timber
     toes,
Because women in the upper storeys demand a face at the
     pane,
That patching old heels they may shriek, I take to chisel and
     plane.

Malachi Stilt-Jack am I, whatever I learned has run wild,
From collar to collar, from stilt to stilt, from father to child.
All metaphor, Malachi, stilts and all. A barnacle goose
Far up in the stretches of night; night splits and the dawn
     breaks loose;
I, through the terrible novelty of light, stalk on, stalk on;
Those great sea-horses bare their teeth and laugh at the dawn.

WHY SHOULD NOT OLD MEN BE MAD?

WHY should not old men be mad?
Some have known a likely lad
That had a sound fly-fisher's wrist
Turn to a drunken journalist;
A girl that knew all Dante once
Live to bear children to a dunce;
A Helen of social welfare dream,
Climb on a wagonette to scream.
Some think it a matter of course that chance
Should starve good men and bad advance,

That if their neighbours figured plain,
As though upon a lighted screen,
No single story would they find
Of an unbroken happy mind,
A finish worthy of the start.
Young men know nothing of this sort,
Observant old men know it well;
And when they know what old books tell,
And that no better can be had,
Know why an old man should be mad.

THE CIRCUS ANIMALS' DESERTION

I

I SOUGHT a theme and sought for it in vain,
I sought it daily for six weeks or so.
Maybe at last, being but a broken man,
I must be satisfied with my heart, although
Winter and summer till old age began
My circus animals were all on show,
Those stilted boys, that burnished chariot,
Lion and woman and the Lord knows what.

II

What can I but enumerate old themes?
First that sea-rider Oisin led by the nose
Through three enchanted islands, allegorical dreams,
Vain gaiety, vain battle, vain repose,
Themes of the embittered heart, or so it seems,
That might adorn old songs or courtly shows;
But what cared I that set him on to ride,
I, starved for the bosom of his faery bride?

And then a counter-truth filled out its play,
The Countess Cathleen was the name I gave it;
She, pity-crazed, had given her soul away,
But masterful Heaven had intervened to save it.
I thought my dear must her own soul destroy,
So did fanaticism and hate enslave it,
And this brought forth a dream and soon enough
This dream itself had all my thought and love.

And when the Fool and Blind Man stole the bread
Cuchulain fought the ungovernable sea;
Heart-mysteries there, and yet when all is said
It was the dream itself enchanted me:
Character isolated by a deed
To engross the present and dominate memory.
Players and painted stage took all my love,
And not those things that they were emblems of.

III

Those masterful images because complete
Grew in pure mind, but out of what began?
A mound of refuse or the sweepings of a street,
Old kettles, old bottles, and a broken can,
Old iron, old bones, old rags, that raving slut
Who keeps the till. Now that my ladder's gone,
I must lie down where all the ladders start,
In the foul rag-and-bone shop of the heart.

POLITICS

*'In our time the destiny of man presents its meaning
in political terms.'*—THOMAS MANN

How can I, that girl standing there,
My attention fix
On Roman or on Russian
Or on Spanish politics?
Yet here's a travelled man that knows
What he talks about,
And there's a politician
That has read and thought,
And maybe what they say is true
Of war and war's alarms,
But O that I were young again
And held her in my arms!

THE MAN AND THE ECHO

Man

In a cleft that's christened Alt
Under broken stone I halt
At the bottom of a pit
That broad noon has never lit,
And shout a secret to the stone.
All that I have said and done,
Now that I am old and ill,
Turns into a question till

I lie awake night after night
And never get the answers right.
Did that play of mine send out
Certain men the English shot?
Did words of mine put too great strain
On that woman's reeling brain?
Could my spoken words have checked
That whereby a house lay wrecked?
And all seems evil until I
Sleepless would lie down and die.

Echo

Lie down and die.

Man

        That were to shirk
The spiritual intellect's great work,
And shirk it in vain. There is no release
In a bodkin or disease,
Nor can there be work so great
As that which cleans man's dirty slate.
While man can still his body keep
Wine or love drug him to sleep,
Waking he thanks the Lord that he
Has body and its stupidity,
But body gone he sleeps no more,
And till his intellect grows sure
That all's arranged in one clear view,
Pursues the thoughts that I pursue,
Then stands in judgment on his soul,
And, all work done, dismisses all
Out of intellect and sight
And sinks at last into the night.

Echo

Into the night.

Man

O Rocky Voice,
Shall we in that great night rejoice?
What do we know but that we face
One another in this place?
But hush, for I have lost the theme,
Its joy or night seem but a dream;
Up there some hawk or owl has struck,
Dropping out of sky or rock.
A stricken rabbit is crying out,
And its cry distracts my thought.

UNDER BEN BULBEN

I

SWEAR by what the sages spoke
Round the Mareotic Lake
That the Witch of Atlas knew,
Spoke and set the cocks a-crow.

Swear by those horsemen, by those women
Complexion and form prove superhuman,
That pale, long-visaged company
That air in immortality
Completeness of their passions won;
Now they ride the wintry dawn
Where Ben Bulben sets the scene.

Here's the gist of what they mean.

II

Many times man lives and dies
Between his two eternities,
That of race and that of soul,
And ancient Ireland knew it all.
Whether man die in his bed
Or the rifle knocks him dead,
A brief parting from those dear
Is the worst man has to fear.
Though grave-diggers' toil is long,
Sharp their spades, their muscles strong,
They but thrust their buried men
Back in the human mind again.

III

You that Mitchel's prayer have heard,
'Send war in our time, O Lord!'
Know that when all words are said
And a man is fighting mad,
Something drops from eyes long blind,
He completes his partial mind,
For an instant stands at ease,
Laughs aloud, his heart at peace.
Even the wisest man grows tense
With some sort of violence
Before he can accomplish fate,
Know his work or choose his mate.

IV

Poet and sculptor, do the work,
Nor let the modish painter shirk

What his great forefathers did,
Bring the soul of man to God,
Make him fill the cradles right.

Measurement began our might:
Forms a stark Egyptian thought,
Forms that gentler Phidias wrought.
Michael Angelo left a proof
On the Sistine Chapel roof,
Where but half-awakened Adam
Can disturb globe-trotting Madam
Till her bowels are in heat,
Proof that there's a purpose set
Before the secret working mind:
Profane perfection of mankind.

Quattrocento put in paint
On backgrounds for a God or Saint
Gardens where a soul's at ease;
Where everything that meets the eye,
Flowers and grass and cloudless sky,
Resemble forms that are or seem
When sleepers wake and yet still dream,
And when it's vanished still declare,
With only bed and bedstead there,
That heavens had opened.

      Gyres run on;
When that greater dream had gone
Calvert and Wilson, Blake and Claude,
Prepared a rest for the people of God,
Palmer's phrase, but after that
Confusion fell upon our thought.

V

Irish poets, learn your trade,
Sing whatever is well made,
Scorn the sort now growing up
All out of shape from toe to top,
Their unremembering hearts and heads
Base-born products of base beds.
Sing the peasantry, and then
Hard-riding country gentlemen,
The holiness of monks, and after
Porter-drinkers' randy laughter;
Sing the lords and ladies gay
That were beaten into the clay
Through seven heroic centuries;
Cast your mind on other days
That we in coming days may be
Still the indomitable Irishry.

VI

Under bare Ben Bulben's head
In Drumcliff churchyard Yeats is laid.
An ancestor was rector there
Long years ago, a church stands near,
By the road an ancient cross.
No marble, no conventional phrase;
On limestone quarried near the spot
By his command these words are cut:

> Cast a cold eye
> On life, on death.
> Horseman, pass by!

September 4, 1938

NOTES

ABBREVIATIONS

A W. B. Yeats, *Autobiographies* (1955)
AV(A) W. B. Yeats, *A Vision* (1925)
AV(B) W. B. Yeats, *A Vision* (1937)
CP (1933; 1950) W. B. Yeats, *Collected Poems*
E & I W. B. Yeats, *Essays and Introductions* (1961)
ISW W. B. Yeats, *In the Seven Woods* (1903)
M W. B. Yeats, *Mythologies* (1959)
WR W. B. Yeats, *The Wind among the Reeds* (1899)
NC A. Norman Jeffares, *A New Commentary on the Poems of W. B. Yeats* (1984)
YANB A. Norman Jeffares, *W. B. Yeats: A New Biography* (1988)
CK *The Countess Kathleen and Various Legends and Lyrics* (1892)
VE *The Variorum Edition of the Poems of W. B. Yeats*, edited by Peter Allt and Russell K. Alspach (1917)

CROSSWAYS

p. 7 *Down by the Salley Gardens* is an attempt to reconstruct an old song from three lines Yeats remembered an old peasant woman singing in the village of Ballisodare, Co. Sligo. The salley gardens (of willow used in thatching roofs) were probably those on the banks of the Ballisodare River in Co. Sligo.

p. 7 *The Ballad of Moll Magee* was suggested by a sermon heard in Howth, Dublin; it was probably written when Yeats was seventeen. The salting shed was on one of the piers on Howth harbour. Kinsale is a fishing port in Co. Cork. Boreen is an Irish word meaning a small road. Keening is uttering the lament for the dead (from the Irish *caoinim*, I wail).

THE ROSE

p. 10 *To the Rose upon the Rood of Time* Yeats used the rose as a symbol for Ireland and Maud Gonne, and also for some of the

209

210   SELECTED POETRY

teachings of a mystical society, the Hermetic Order of the Golden
Dawn, of which he was a member (the conjoined Rose and Cross,
for instance, symbolized a mystic marriage). In general, the rose
also stood for spiritual and eternal beauty in his early poetry. This
poem also contains imagery from the Gaelic legends, Cuchulain
being the hero of the Ulster cycle of tales, who, not knowing his
identity, kills his own son and dies fighting the sea. Fergus was the
king of Ulster, leader of the Red Branch heroes; he was tricked by
his wife Ness into giving the throne to her son Conchubar (or
Conor), his step-son.

p. 11 *Fergus and the Druid* According to Sir Samuel Ferguson's ver-
sion of the legend which Yeats is using here, Fergus gave up his
throne to live at peace hunting in the woods. A quern is an appar-
atus (usually two circular stones) for grinding corn.

p. 12 *Cuchulain's Fight with the Sea* Emer was Cuchulain's wife; his
'young sweetheart' was Eithne Inguba. This poem is founded upon
a West of Ireland legend given in Jeremiah Curtin's *Myths and
Folklore of Ireland* (1890).

p. 16 *The Lake Isle of Innisfree* Innisfree is an island associated with
local legends in Lough Gill, Co. Sligo, where Yeats, influenced by
Thoreau's *Walden*, dreamed of living alone in search of wisdom.
The poem was written in London in 1890.

p. 17 *The Sorrow of Love*, first written in October 1891, was rewrit-
ten several times by Yeats; it first appeared in *CK*. The different
revisions can be found in *VE*, p. 119. The girl who arose is pre-
sumably Helen of Troy. Wife of Menelaus, King of Sparta, she ran
away to Troy with Paris, a son of Priam, King of Troy. This caused
the Trojan war, in which the Greeks besieged the city and finally
sacked it, having entered it by the ruse of the wooden horse. This
was suggested by Odysseus, one of the Greek leaders. The *Odyssey*
tells of his adventures and the tribulations he suffered during the ten
years it took him to return to Ithaca after the fall of Troy. Priam did
not survive the sack of the city; the classical account tells of his
seeking refuge at the altar of Zeus Herkeios in his palace, where he
was killed by Neoptolemus, the son of Achilles. When Yeats wrote
of Helen of Troy he was using her as a means of praising Maud
Gonne's beauty.

p. 17 *When You are Old* is founded upon 'Quand vous serez bien vieille' by Pierre de Ronsard (1524–5); it is one of his *Sonnets pour Hélène* II (1578). It was written to Maud Gonne.

p. 18 *The White Birds* was written after Maud Gonne had spent a day with Yeats walking on the cliffs at Howth (the peninsula that forms the northern arm of Dublin Bay); two seagulls flew over their heads and on out to sea, which prompted Maud Gonne to say to Yeats that if she was to have the choice of being a bird she would choose to be a seagull. He sent her the poems three days later. In its first printing, in the *National Observer*, 7 May 1892, a note explained that the birds of fairyland are said to be as white as snow. The meteor is mentioned because of the brevity of its existence in the eye of the beholder; the blue star of the twilight is Venus. The lily and rose are, respectively, masculine and feminine symbols. In *CK* Yeats commented that the Danaan Shore is Tir-nan-oge, or fairyland. (*Tir na nOg* in Irish means the Land of the Young, where mortals could share the everlasting youth of the fairies.) 'Yeats's note in *WR* stated that the powerful and wealthy called the gods of ancient Ireland the Tuatha De Danaan, or Tribes of the goddess Danu [the mother of the gods] but the poor called them, and sometimes still call them, the Sidhe [pronounced Shee]; from Aes Sidhe or Sluagh Sidhe, the people of the Fairy Hills, as these words are explained. Sidhe is also Gaelic for wind and certainly the Sidhe have much to do with the wind. They journey in whirling winds that were ca lled the dance of the daughters of Herodias in the Middle Ages, Herodias doubtless taking the place of some old goddess. When the country people see the leaves whirling on the road they bless themselves, because they believe the Sidhe to be passing by.'

p. 19 *The Man who dreamed of faeryland* This poem is set in Co. Leitrim and Co. Sligo. Dromahair is a village in Co. Leitrim on the river Bonnet which flows into Logh Gill. See *M*, pp. 5 and 70. Its Irish name means the Ridge of the Two Demons. The world-forgotten isle is akin to the first paradisaical place to which the fairy princess brings Oisin in Yeats's *The Wanderings of Oisin* (1889). Lissadell (the Irish means the fort of the blind man) is a barony in Co. Sligo. Lissadell was the name of the house built in 1832–4 by the Gore-Booth family, who have lived in the area since the early eighteenth century (see 'In Memory of Eva Gore-Booth and Con Markiewicz', p. 141). The money cares and fears probably refer to Yeats's lack of friends as a young man when he spent summers in Sligo with his Pollexfen grandparents and his uncle George Pollexfen. The hill is the hill of Lugnagall (see l. 37). Yeats described it in a story 'The Curse of the Fires and the Shadows' (see *M* p. 182) as an abyss or, in English, the steep place of the strangers [it should be translated as the Hollow of the Strangers]. Lugnagall is a townland in the Glencar Valley, Co. Sligo. The golden or silver skies are solar and lunar principles; when fused they are an alchemical emblem of perfection. A dancer represents fairyland and a state of blessedness. The sun and moon echo the golden and silver skies of l. 21. There is a well at Scanavin (in Irish it is called the Well of fine Shingle) a mile from Colloney, Co. Sligo. Scanavin is also the name of a townland in Co. Sligo. The stormy silver and the gold of day re-echo the imagery of *ll*. 21 and 23. The word 'Spiring' anticipates the movement described in 'Demon and Beast' (see p. 98). It is also used in 'The Two Trees' (see p. 20).

p. 20 *The Two Trees* The holy tree is the Sephirotic tree of the Kabbalah and the tree of knowledge. The tree has two aspects, one of them benign, the other malign. The Tree of Life was described by Yeats as a geometrical figure made up of ten circles of Spheres called Sephiroth joined by straight lines. See *A*, p. 375. The bitter glass is the tree in its malign aspect. Yeats read about the tree in MacGregor Mathers *The Kabbalah Unveiled* (1887). There it was the Tree of Knowledge of Good and Evil; the birds built their nests in its branches and the souls and the angels had their places in it also (see *E&I* p. 44). The demons probably symbolise abstract thought, ambushing the soul on its road to truth. A fatal image is the Tree of Knowledge as opposed to the Tree of Life (see *E&I* pp. 28–52 and, particularly, p. 130).

p. 22 *To Ireland in the Coming Times* This poem partly defends some of the obscurity caused by Yeats's interest in mysticism and occultism, 'a passion for the symbolism of the mystical rose which has saddened my friends' and partly explains his attitude to the role of literature in shaping Ireland's struggle for independence. It is also a love poem to Maud Gonne. She wanted direct political action; he is saying his work continues and develops that of earlier Irish writers. Thomas Davis (1814–45), who founded the *Nation* in 1842, a journal which had a profound influence in Ireland, was a leader of the Young Ireland party and wrote poems and prose of a popular patriotic nature; James Clarence Mangan (1803–49), a romantic Irish poet and essayist, wrote prolifically in magazines and journals, adapting Irish and German originals; and Sir Samuel Ferguson (1810–86), an Irish lawyer, poet and antiquary rendered Gaelic legends in a masculine manner; he also wrote some very effective lyrics, among them the 'Lament for Thomas Davis'. Yeats's rhymes more than their rhyming tell because he was trying to blend Christian and pagan material and to incorporate occult imagery and ideas, his symbolism thus creating a touch of mystery (which made his poetry obscure: the original title of the poem was 'Apologia addressed to Ireland in the Coming Days').

p. 24 *The Hosting of the Sidhe* For the Sidhe see note on 'The White Birds', p. 211. The locations are in Sligo. Knocknarea is in Co. Sligo. Yeats's note in *WR* commented, 'The country people say that Maeve, still a great queen of the western Sidhe, is buried in the cairn of stones upon it.' He went on to say that he had written of Clooth-na-Bare in *The Celtic Twilight* and that she 'went all over the world seeking a lake deep enough to drown her fairy life, of which she had grown weary, leaping from hill to hill, and setting up a cairn of stones wherever her feet lighted, until, at last, she found the deepest water in the world in little Lough Ia [Irish, *Loch da Ghe*, the Lake of the Two Geese], on the top of the bird mountain, in Sligo'. He thought he might have got the story from a priest in Collooney; it may have come from W. G. Wood-Martin's *History of Sligo County and Town* (1882–92) III, p. 354, or his *Pagan Ireland: an Archeological Sketch* (1895), p. 126. Yeats's note continued with an explanation of the name Clooth-na-Bare, which would, he said, mean the old woman of Bare, but is evidently a corruption of Cailleac Bare, the old woman Bare, who under the names Bare, and Berah, and Beri, and Verah, and Dera, and Dhira, appears in the legends of many places. [The Veiled Woman or Hag of Beare, in Co. Cork, is the speaker in a nineteeth-century poem; she laments her lost youth, her present decay and decrepitude; the poem can be taken as an old nun's lament or as a symbol of Christian Ireland remembering her pagan past.] Mr O'Grady found her haunting

Lough Liath high up on the top of a mountain of Fews [in Co. Armagh], the Slieve Fuadh, or Slieve G-Cullain of old times, under the name of the Cailleac Buillia. He describes Lough Liath as a desolate moon-shaped lake, with made wells and sunken passages upon its borders, and beset by marsh and heather and grey boulders, and closes his 'Flight of the Eagle' [1897; see pp. 255-7 and 296-7] with a long rhapsody upon mountain and lake, because of the heroic tales and beautiful old myths that have hung about them always. He identifies the Cailleac Buillia with that Meluchra who persuaded Fionn to go to her amid the waters of Lough Liath, and so changed him with her enchantments, that, though she had to free him because of the threats of the Fiana, his hair was ever afterwards as white as snow. To this day, the Tribes of the Goddess Danu that are in the waters beckon to men, and drown them in the waters; and Bare, or Dhira, or Meluchra, or whatever name one likes the best, is, doubtless, the name of a mistress among them. Meluchra was daughter of Cullain; and Cullain Mr O'Grady calls, upon I know not what authority, a form of Lir, the master of waters. The people of the waters have been in all ages beautiful and changeable and lascivious, or beautiful and wise and lonely, for water is everywhere the signature of the fruitfulness of the body and of the fruitfulness of dreams. The white hair of Fionn may be but another of the troubles of those that come to unearthly wisdom and earthly trouble, and the threats and violence of the Fiana against her a different form of the threats and violence the country people use, to make the Tribes of Danu give up those that are 'away'. Bare is now often called an ugly old woman; but Dr Joyce says that one of her old names was Aebhin, which means beautiful. Aebhen was the goddess of the tribes of northern Leinster; and the lover she had made immortal, and who loved her perfectly, left her, and put on mortality, to fight among them against the stranger, and died on the strand of Clontarf.' Caoilte and his burning hair were explained in the notes to *WR*. A comrade of Oisin, the son of Finn (whose doings are told in the Fenian cycle of Gaelic tales, which probably generally date from the twelfth century, though same may have been composed in the eighth century), he was one of 'the great of the old times' who were treated as kings and queens among the Tribes of Danu. Years after his death he appeared to a king in a forest, and was a flaming man that he might lead him in the darkness. When the king asked him who he was, he said, 'I am your candlestick.' Niamh was 'a beautiful woman of the Tribes of Danu, that led Oisin to the Country of the Young'. He stayed there with her for three centuries; their adventures are told in Yeats's *The Wanderings of Oisin* of 1889.

p. 24 *The Lover tells of the Rose in his Heart* This is a love poem to Maud Gonne.

p. 25 *The Host of the Air* is founded upon an old Gaelic ballad Yeats heard sung in Ballisodare, Co. Sligo. In it the husband found the keeners (See note on 'The Ballad of Moll Magee', p.209) keening for his wife when he got home. Yeats used the same ballad material in his story 'Kidnapped' (*M*, 73ff). Hart Lake is in the Ox Mountains, six or seven miles west of Ballisodare in Co. Sligo.

p. 27 *The Unappeasable Host* The Danaan children are the Tuatha de Danaan, or Gods of ancient Ireland. A ger-eagle is a kind of vulture, the word geier-eagle being used to translate the Hebrew *raham* in the Bible. (See Lev. xi. 18 and Deut. xiv. 7).

p. 27 *The Song of Wandering Aengus* Aengus is the Irish god of beauty and poetry, who reigned in Tir nan Oge, the Country of the Young. The glimmering girl is probably an image of Maud Gonne, associated in Yeats's mind with apple blossom (see *A* p.123). The poem was suggested to him, Yeats commented in *WR*, by a Greek folk song, though when he wrote it he was thinking of Ireland 'and of the spirits that are in Ireland'. For a discussion of sources of the poem see Jeffares, *NC*, pp. 52–3.

p. 28 *He mourns for the Change that has come upon him and his Beloved and longs for the End of the World* The white deer with no horns and the hound with one red ear Yeats found in 'a last-century Gaelic poem about Oisin's journey to the country of the young'. He thought hound and deer images of the desire of the man 'which is for the woman' and 'the desire of the woman which is for the desire of the man'. The man with the hazel wand is Aengus, the Master of Love, and the Boar without bristles comes out of the west because that is a place of symbolic darkness and death in Irish belief. Yeats refers to Irish country people's prophetic visions of a great battle to be fought (in a mysterious Valley of the Black Pig), which would break the power of their enemies. He thought of it as a mythological battle and wrote a long note to this effect in *WR*. See 'The Valley of the Black Pig', p. 32 and notes on it below.

p. 29 *He bids his Beloved be at Peace* Yeats remarked in his notes to *WR* that November was associated by Irish people with the horse-shaped Púcas who, he thought, might have connections with the horses of the sea-god Mannannan Mac Lir who ruled over the country of the dead. Though they 'could cross the land as easily as the sea, [they] are constantly associated with the waves. Some Neo-platonist, I forget who, describes the sea as a symbol of the drifting indefinite bitterness of life, and I believe there is live symbolism intended in the many Irish voyages to the isles of enchantment, or that there was, at any rate, in the mythology out of which these stories have been shaped. I follow much Irish and other mythology, and the magical tradition, in associating the North with night and sleep, and the East, the place of sunrise, with hope, and the South, the place of the sun when at its height, with passion and desire, and the West, the place of sunset, with fading and dreaming things'.

p. 31 *The Cap and Bells* is a memory of a dream.

p. 32 *The Valley of the Black Pig* In a note Yeats related this poem to Irish prophecies of the rout of Ireland's enemies in the Valley of the Black Pig. See note above on 'He mourns . . . End of the World'. Later, however, he thought it might have been inspired by talk of MacGregor Mathers. Mathers, a student of the occult who had enrolled Yeats in the Order of the Golden Dawn in 1890, thought that apocalyptic wars would occur at the end of the nine-teenth century.

p. 33 *The Secret Rose* Yeats had a half-belief that there would be a revelation when an Order of Celtic mysteries had been established; he foresaw it embodying a philosophy part Christian, part pagan, an idea this poem expresses. The Rose, with its four leaves, was a Rosicrucian emblem. (It can also symbolize Ireland and Maud Gonne in Yeats's poetry.) Yeats described the Rose as for many years a symbol of spiritual love and supreme beauty. The Holy Sepulchre is Christ's tomb in Jerusalem. The Magi are the three wise men who came from the East to attend Christ's birth, bringing gifts of gold, frankincense and myrrh. The King is Conchubar, who when told of the crucifixion of Jesus Christ (conveyed by the

Pierced Hands and the Rood [the cross] of Elder) said that he would kill those who were putting Christ to death. He hacked in fury at a grove of trees with his sword to show how he would do this, and died when a ball made out of the brain of a dead enemy which had lodged in his head after an earlier battle 'started out of it and some of the brain came after it'. Cuchulain, one of the Red Branch heroes, met Fand (the wife of the sea god Mannannan Mac Lir) who loved him. He spent a month with her in the Country of the gods, then promised to meet her at 'the Yew at the Strand's End', but Emer, his mortal wife, won his love again, so it was Manannan, not Cuchulain, who met Fand at the Yew and carried her away. The man who drove the gods from their liss, or fort, was the hero Caoilte MacRonan. The proud dreaming king was Fergus, and the man who sold his property was derived from a tale in William Larminie, *West Irish Folk Tales and Romances* (1893).

IN THE SEVEN WOODS

p 38 *The Arrow* is a memory of Yeats's first meeting with Maud Gonne in January 1889.

p. 39 *Red Hanrahan's Song about Ireland* is written to Maud Gonne (who played Cathleen, who symbolizes Ireland, in Yeats's play *Cathleen ni Houlihan* in 1902). It was extensively revised; the first version of 1894 is given in A. Norman Jeffares, *YANB*, p. 87. Cummen (Irish *caimin*, the little common) Strand is to the north-west of Sligo, on the road to Strandhill. Knocknarea (in Irish the Mountain of the Kings) overlooks Sligo. Yeats commented that the country people believed that Maeve, 'still a great queen of the Western Sidhe', was buried in the cairn of stones on the top of it. In the Ulster (Red Branch) cycle of tales she was the Queen of Connaught and began the war described in the epic tale, the *Tain Bo Cualgne*. Clooth-na-Bare is Lough Ia, on the top of the Birds' Mountain in Co. Sligo.

p. 39 *Under the Moon* Brycelinde was the forest of Broceliande in Brittany where Viviane bewitched Merlin. Avalon was a mythical land in the Isles of the Blessed where King Arthur was brought after his death. Joyous Isle was a place in the prose *Lancelot*. Lancelot, lover of Queen Guinevere, found Arthur was dead and his widow had taken the veil. He became a priest, guarded Arthur's grave, and

when he died was carried to Joyous Gard. (Lancelot had lived in
Joyous Isle with Elayne after her friend Dame Brysen had cured
him of his madness.) Ulad/Uladh is Ulster, the northern of
Ireland's four provinces. Naoise, son of Usna, carried off Deirdre
(whom Conchubar intended to marry) to Scotland and was eventu-
ally killed, with his two brothers, through treachery on the part of
Conchubar, when he and Deirdre and his brothers came back to
Ireland under a safe conduct. Land-under-Wave is a name (Irish,
Tir-fa-Thon) for the magic underworld under the sea. The seven old
sisters may be the planets, but are more likely to be the Pleiades, the
seven daughters, in Greek mythology, of Atlas. Land-of-the-
Tower is probably the house of glass belonging to Aengus, where
Edain, wife of Midhir (a king of the Sidhe) came in a fit of jealousy
to live with Aengus. Wood-of-Wonders is the Forest of Wonders in
'The Tale of the Adventures of the King of Norway' (it was edited
by Douglas Hyde for the first volume issued by the Irish Texts
Society in 1899). The ox was killed by the hero Cod, who later saw
it borne on a golden bier by a 'fair bevy of women' led by 'a
high-headed sensible queen'. Branwen, the daughter of Llyr, was
the wife of Matholwych, King of Ireland in the *Mabinogion*, which
Yeats read in Lady Charlotte Guest's translation. For Niamh see
note on 'The Hosting of the Sidhe', p. 213. Laban (Irish *Li-Ban*,
woman's beauty) was a sister of Fand: see note on 'The Secret
Rose', p. 216. The wood-woman is from 'The Tale of the Adven-
tures of the King of Norway'; her lover was turned into a hawk by
the daughter of the King of Greece. Dun is the Irish word for a fort.

p. 40 *O do not love too long* The poem was written to Maud Gonne,
who 'changed' after her marriage in 1903.

p. 41 *The Happy Townland* Yeats remarked that the poem sym-
bolized striving after an impossible ideal. Michael is the archangel,
described elsewhere by Yeats as having the trumpet of the Last
Judgment (a role usually allotted to the archangel Gabriel). In this
poem Gabriel comes from the water, probably because Yeats,
describing him as the Angel of the Moon in the Cabbala (a Jewish
mystical tradition based upon esoteric interpretation of the Old
Testament), considered he might 'command the waters, at a pinch'.

THE GREEN HELMET AND OTHER POEMS

pp. 44 and 45 *Words, No Second Troy* and *Reconciliation* are addressed to Maud Gonne, who married John MacBride in 1903, to Yeats's great distress. The marriage resulted in a separation two years later.

p. 44 *Words* This is based on a prose passage in a 1908 diary in which Yeats wrote that Maud Gonne 'never really understands my plans, or nature or ideas . . . How much of the best I have done and still do is but the attempt to explain myself to her? If she understood I should lack a reason for writing, and one can never have too many reasons for doing what is so laborious.' She did not 'understand' his refusal to make his art into political propaganda.

p. 44 *No Second Troy* Here Yeats refers to the violent ways Maud Gonne advocated at committee meetings, in articles and in speeches. She was deeply involved in anti-British activities, had been a member of the Irish Republican Brotherhood, which she had linked with French Military Intelligence, and had suggested to a Boer agent in Brussels a plan for placing bombs in British troopships bound for South Africa. In referring to the fall of Troy, which the Greeks burnt after their ten-year siege of the city, Yeats is comparing Maud to Helen, who caused the Trojan war by leaving her husband Menelaus, King of Sparta, for Paris, son of King Priam of Troy, who brought her back to Troy with him.

p. 45 *Reconciliation* describes the immediate effect of Maud Gonne's marriage on Yeats when, 'ears . . . deafened; sight . . . blind', he heard the news just before he was to give a lecture. He never remembered what he said (it was apparently a very good lecture), and afterwards walked the streets aimlessly for hours in great misery. The helmets, crowns and swords probably refer to his heroic plays *The King's Threshhold* and *On Baile's Strand*. The pit is not a theatre pit but a hole in the ground, a grave for the plays.

p. 46 *The Mask* First written in Yeats's diary, this became a lyric in his play *The Player Queen* (1922). In the play the man speaks *ll.* 1–2, 6–7, 11–12, and the woman replies.

p. 46 *Upon a House Shaken by the Land Agitation* refers to Coole Park, the Gregory house and estate in Galway. The lidless eye echoes a belief that only an eagle can stare into the sun without blinking. The eagle thoughts symbolize those of active, objective persons. Mean roof-trees allude to the cottages or small farmhouses whose inhabitants would benefit from reductions in land rents. Yeats's diary included a prose draft of the poem and an explanation of it.

> Subject for a Poem. A Shaken House. How should the world gain if this house failed, even though a hundred little houses were the better for it, for here power has gone forth, or lingered giving energy, precision; it gives to a far people beneficent rule [Lady Gregory's husband, Sir William Gregory, had been governor of Ceylon]; and still under its roof loving intellect is sweetened by old memories of its descents from far off; how should the world be better if the wren's nest flourish and the eagle's house is scattered?

The explanation read:

> I wrote this poem on hearing the result of reduction of rent made by the courts. One feels that when all must make their living they will live not for life's sake but the work's and all be the poorer. My work is very near to life itself and my father's very near to life itself but I am always feeling a lack of life's own values behind my thought. They should have been there before the stream began, before it became necessary to let the work create its values. This house has enriched my soul out of measure because here life moves within restraint through gracious forms. Here there has been no compelled labour, no poverty-thwarted impulse.

p. 47 *All Things can Tempt me.* Yeats wrote little verse while he was Manager of the Abbey Theatre (1904–10).

RESPONSIBILITIES

p. 49 *Introductory Rhymes* were provoked by the Irish novelist George Moore's remarks on Yeats's family background in *Vale*, the last volume of his autobiographical *Hail and Farewell*, an account of his days in Dublin in the early days of the Irish theatre from 1901 to 1911. Yeats finished *Reveries*, the first part of his Autobiographies, in 1914, regarding it as 'some sort of apologia for the Yeats family', and this poem was written between 1912 and 1914, when he had become interested in his ancestry. The old Dublin merchant was possibly Jervis Yeats (d. 1712), the first of the Yeatses to settle in Ireland (he came from Yorkshire) or, more likely, his grandson Benjamin (1750–95), a linen merchant like his father and grandfather. He was free of six and ten per cent taxes levied in Dublin. (Yeats later realized that 'ten and four' was wrong.) The old country scholar was Yeats's great-grandfather, Rev. John Yeats (1776–1846), rector of Drumcliff, Co. Sligo. A Butler is mentioned because Benjamin Yeats married into this powerful and distinguished ducal Anglo-Irish family, and the Yeatses, valuing the connection, frequently used Butler as a Christian name from then on. An Armstrong refers to a connection with a military family; the poet's grandfather, Rev. William Butler Yeats (1806–62), married Jane Grace Corbet, whose mother was born Grace Armstrong. The Battle of the Boyne (1690) marked the defeat of James II by William of Orange (William III). The old merchant skipper was William Middleton, the poet's maternal great-grandfather; the fierce old man his maternal grandfather, William Pollexfen (1811–92), a retired sea captain and merchant who lived in Sligo and had married Elizabeth Middleton. Yeats spent several years in their house as a child. The barren passion describes his love for Maud Gonne.

p. 50 *The Grey Rock* The poets, members of the Rhymers' Club (founded by Yeats and Ernest Rhys in 1890), who met in The Cheshire Cheese in Fleet Street, London, in the nineties, were, many of them, interested in Celtic literature; they included Lionel Johnson (1867–1902), Ernest Dowson (1867–1900), and Arthur Symons (1865–1945).

p. 50 *To a Wealthy Man who promised a Second Subscription to the Dublin Municipal Gallery if it were proved the People wanted Pictures.* Sir Hugh Lane offered his pictures to Dublin if they were properly housed, but in disgust at Dublin's reception of the gift placed the pictures in the National Gallery, London. Before going down in the *Lusitania* (which was torpedoed by a U-boat off the Irish coast in 1915) he had added an unwitnessed codicil to his will leaving the pictures to Dublin. The pictures remained in London until a recent agreement which shares them between Dublin and London.

p. 55 *September 1913* John O'Leary (1830–1907), a Fenian leader sentenced to twenty years' hard labour in 1865, was released under an amnesty after serving five years on condition that he kept out of Ireland. He spent fifteen years in Paris and returned to Ireland in 1885. He greatly influenced Yeats as a young man. The wild geese was a name given to Irishmen who (because of the Penal Laws passed after 1691 which prevented their holding commissions in the British army) served abroad, notably in the Irish Brigade in the French army. Others fought for the Swedish army. About 120,000 wild geese left Ireland between 1690 and 1730. Lord Edward Fitzgerald joined the United Irishmen in 1796; he died of wounds received when he was being arrested. Robert Emmet led an abortive revolt in 1803; he was hanged for high treason. Theobald Wolfe Tone, founder of the United Club, became a *chef-de-brigade* in France and led a French force to Ireland. Captured at Lough Swilly, he was condemned to death by a court martial and committed suicide in prison.

p. 57 *To a Shade* is addressed to Charles Stewart Parnell (1846–91), the Irish parliamentary leader repudiated by Gladstone, the Irish Hierarchy and the Irish Party because of his affair with Mrs O'Shea. He is buried in Glasnevin Cemetery, Dublin, and a monument was erected to him in O'Connell Street. The man of his own kind is Sir Hugh Lane. His enemy is William Martin Murphy, proprietor of two Dublin newspapers, who opposed Lane's gift of his pictures to Dublin. Murphy had earlier led the attack on Parnell.

p. 60 *The Mountain Tomb* Yeats wrote an essay in which he described the tradition that the followers of Father Christian Rosencrux, who reputedly founded the Rosicrucian Order in 1484, wrapped his body in imperishable raiment and put it in a tomb containing symbols of all things in heaven, earth and the waters under the earth, and placed inextinguishable magic lamps around his body, which burnt on generation after generation until some students of the Order came upon the tomb by chance (see *E & I*, pp. 196 ff).

p. 60 *To a Child dancing in the Wind* This poem was written about Iseult Gonne (1894–1954), Maud Gonne's daughter by Lucien Millevoye. It was set in Normandy, and was written at Les Mouettes, Maud Gonne's house at Colleville, near Calvados.

p. 61 *Friends* The poem, written in 1911, describes in turn Mrs Shakespear (1867–1938), Lady Gregory (1859–1932) and Maud

Gonne (1866–1953). Yeats first met Olivia Shakespear in 1894; he had an affair with her in 1896, a relationship renewed some time after Maud Gonne's marriage, possibly in 1910. When Olivia died Yeats wrote that for more than forty years she was the centre of his life in London and that during that time they never had a quarrel, 'sadness perhaps, but never a difference'. Lady Gregory, whom he met briefly in London in 1894 and visited briefly in 1896 at Coole Park, Co. Galway (where he spent the next summer, the first of many long annual visits up to his marriage), realized the strains imposed by his long unsuccessful wooing of Maud Gonne, renewed his interest in folklore and helped him to create the Irish theatre movement at a time when he thought this virtually impossible, a mere dream. Their joint enthusiasm and activity led to the foundation of the Abbey Theatre in Dublin. The labouring in ecstasy refers to her effect on his writing. He recorded how he had requested her 'to send me to my work every day . . . rating me with idleness if need be, and I doubt if I should have done much with my life but for her firmness and care' (A, p. 377). Maud Gonne 'took all' until his youth was gone; he was in love with her from 1889 on, when he was twenty-three; she married John MacBride in 1903, when Yeats was thirty-seven.

p. 62 *Appointment* The poem records Yeats's disappointment and annoyance that Count Plunkett, not Sir Hugh Lane, was appointed as Curator of the National Museum in Dublin.

p. 63 *The Magi* This is the first of Yeats's poems to carry the ideas of *A Vision*; it puts his belief that the Christian revelation was not final, that history runs in opposing movements.

THE WILD SWANS AT COOLE

p. 65 *In Memory of Major Robert Gregory* Major Robert Gregory, Lady Gregory's only son, was killed in action over the Italian front in January 1918. (He was shot down in error by an Italian pilot.) Yeats's 'house' is Thoor Ballylee, the Norman tower in Galway which he bought in 1917 and lived in during summers until 1929. Lionel Johnson (1887–1902) was a minor English poet who impressed Yeats greatly by his assurance and courtesy; they met in 1888 or 1889. In his later years Johnson drank to excess. Yeats met John Millington Synge (1871–1909), the Irish dramatist, poet and essayist, in Paris in 1896 and persuaded him to go to the Aran Islands and give expression to the life of the then remote and isolated Irish-speaking inhabitants. Synge wrote *The Aran Islands* (1907), illustrated by Jack B. Yeats. The plays *Riders to the Sea* and *The Playboy of the Western World* were inspired by his visits to Aran. His plays caused much controversy, among them *In the Shadow of the Glen*, set in Co. Wicklow. *The Playboy of the Western World* was received with rioting when it was produced at the Abbey Theatre in Dublin in 1907. Synge died of Hodgkin's Disease. George Pollexfen (1871–1910), Yeats's hypochondriacal uncle, lived in Sligo (where Yeats occasionally stayed with him as a young man); he was an astrologer and became a member of the Order of the Golden Dawn. Robert Gregory is compared to Sir Philip Sidney (who also died young as a soldier, fighting overseas) because of his Renaissance versatility. Castle Taylor, Roxborough, Esserkelly and Mooneen are placed in Co. Galway; Clare is the county south of Co. Galway.

p. 69 *An Irish Airman Foresees his Death* also concerns Major Robert Gregory. Kiltartan Cross is a crossroads near Coole Park, Co. Galway.

p. 69 *To a Young Beauty* is written to Iseult Gonne. See note on 'To a Child Dancing in the Wind', p. 222. Ezekiel's cherubim are mentioned in Ezekiel *ix.* 3; *x.* 2, 6, 7, 14, 16, 19; *xxviii.* 16 and *xli.* 18. Jacques Firmin Beauvarlet (1731–97) was a mediocre French painter and engraver. Yeats read Walter Savage Landor (1775–1864), a minor English poet, famous for his prose *Conversations*, in the winters of 1914, 1915 and 1916. He read John Donne (1571/2–1631), the metaphysical poet, in 1912, in Professor H. J. C. Grierson's edition.

p. 70 *To a Young Girl* is also written to Iseult Gonne.

p. 71 *The Scholars*. Caius Valerius Catullus (?84–?54 BC) was a famous Roman love poet.

p. 71 *The Fisherman* is a description of an ideal man (*ll.* 1–8), who, Yeats thought, existed in Ireland (*ll.* 9–12); but *ll.* 14–28 describe the 'reality' that he found instead. Connemara is an area in Co. Galway with its western border on the Atlantic.

p. 73 *Her Praise, The People* and *Broken Dreams* refer to Maud Gonne. The unmannerly town in 'The People' is Dublin, which had refused

Sir Hugh Lane's pictures and given a hostile reception to Synge's plays; it is contrasted with the Italian cities whose Renaissance rulers had been enlightened patrons of the arts. The images probably derive from Yeats's visit to Italy with Lady Gregory and her son in 1907, when he visited Urbino and Ferrara and other places, as well as from Castiglione's *The Book of the Courtier*, which describes the ducal court at Urbino. Yeats knew both Hoby's and Opdycke's translations of it.

p. 76 *Presences* The women alluded to in the last three lines of this poem are, respectively, Mabel Dickinson, a well-connected masseuse with whom Yeats had an affair, broken off in 1914; Iseult Gonne (a child) and Maud Gonne (a queen).

p. 77 *Ego Dominus Tuus* The title is from Dante's *Vita Nuova*, in which he sees the Lord of Terrible Aspect in his chamber; this sentence (the Latin means 'I am thy Master') is one of the few he understands. The poem is set in the immediate neighbourhood of Yeats's tower, Ballylee Castle (which he called Thoor Ballylee, from the Irish *tur*, or *thur*, a tower). Michael Robartes and Owen Aherne (in the poem 'The Phases of the Moon') were imaginary characters, who appeared in Yeats's stories of 1897, *Rosa Alchemica*, *The Tables of the Law* and *The Adoration of the Magi* (in *M.*, pp. 267–315). Both also appear in *AV*(A) and *AV*(B). Lapo is either Lapo degli Uberti (son of the Ghibelline leader in Florence, Farinata degli Uberti) or Lapo Gianni; both were friends of Dante. Guido Cavalcanti, the Italian poet, was also one of Dante's friends.

p. 80 *The Phases of the Moon* This poem expounds one of the central ideas in Yeats's *A Vision* and is similar to, complementary to, 'Ego Dominus Tuus' (see notes above). It is also set by Yeats's tower. The phases of the moon are illustrated in *A Vision* (see Select Bibliography p. 243) in a diagram. Milton's Platonist is an allusion to an illustration by Samuel Palmer (1805–81) in an 1889 edition of Milton's *Shorter Poems*, entitled 'The Lonely Tower', the high lonely tower of *Il Penseroso*, *l.* 186. Shelley's visionary prince is Prince Athanase. In his poem of that name Shelley echoed Milton's imagery in *Il Penseroso*. The extravagant style of Walter Pater (1839–94), English essayist and critic, influenced Yeats's involved and decorative prose of the 1890s. Robartes's remark that Yeats said he was dead refers to the story *Rosa Alchemica*, in which he is killed in a riot; his terrible destiny is mentioned in the story *The Tables of the Law* and his death referred to in the story *The Adoration of the Magi*. A cat-o'-nine-tails is a rope whip, of nine knotted thongs, formerly used to flog prisoners. Athene takes Achilles by the hair in Homer's *Iliad*, in Book I. He killed Hector, the eldest of King Priam's sons, in the Trojan war, in revenge for the death of his friend Patroclus (see *Iliad* xxii). Friedrich Nietzsche (1844–1900), a German philosopher, was known for his concept of the superman. Mount Sinai, at the north end of the Red Sea, is where Moses received the Ten Commandments (see Exodus xxxiv and xxxv). The man within the tower is Yeats.

p. 85 *The Cat and the Moon* Minnaloushe was the Gonnes' cat. The idea of the pupils of the cat's eyes changing was probably suggested by a letter written to Yeats by Mrs Felkin (wife of the chief of the Stella Matutina, which derived from the Order of the Golden Dawn after a split in that organization. Yeats and his wife were members of it up to 1922), in which she remarked on a cat's pupils corresponding to the waxing and waning of the moon.

p. 86 *The Double Vision of Michael Robartes* The Rock of Cashel, Co. Tipperary, has several ecclesiastical ruins, including Cormac's ruined chapel, the chapel restored by Cormac McCarthy in the twelfth century. The poem is related closely to *A Vision*, where the cold spirits come from the later Phases of the Moon; the Buddha and Sphinx guard 'the mystery of the fifteenth phase'.

MICHAEL ROBARTES AND THE DANCER

p. 89 *Michael Robartes and the Dancer He* represents Yeats's views, *She* Iseult Gonne's (see note on 'To a Child Dancing in the Wind' p. 222). The altar-piece may be a memory of *Saint George and the Dragon*, a painting ascribed to Bordone (*c.* 1500–1571), in the National Gallery of Ireland, Dublin. Athene was the Greek virgin goddess of wisdom and practical skills. Paul Veronese – the cognomen of Paolo Cagliari (1528–88) – was the last of the great painters of Venice. The lagoon *She* loves so much is the lagoon at Venice. Yeats often visited the Sistine Chapel in the Vatican when he was in Rome in 1925, and greatly admired the paintings on the ceiling by Michaelangelo – Michelangelo Buonarroti (1475–1564). The Latin text referred to may be a Latin translation by Marsilio

Ficino (1433–99) of Plotinus (203–70), the first and most original of the Neoplatonic philosophers.

p. 91 *Solomon and the Witch* is a poem about Yeats and his wife, *née* Georgie Hyde Lees (1892–1968), whom he married in 1917. The Fall is the Fall of Man, when Adam and Eve ate the forbidden fruit, 'the brigand apple', of the Tree of Knowledge. (See Genesis iii.)

p. 92 *Under Saturn* This poem is addressed to Mrs Yeats. Yeats is gloomy and taciturn because of the influence of the planet Saturn. Lost love indicates his love for Maud Gonne. The old cross Pollexfen was Yeats's grandfather, William Pollexfen (1811–92); see notes on 'Introductory Rhymes', p. 220. The Middleton was probably Yeats's great-uncle William Middleton (1806–62) and the red-haired Yeats his grandfather, Rev. William Butler Yeats (1806–62), rector of Tullylish, Co. Down.

p. 93 *Easter 1916* gives Yeats's reactions to the 1916 Rising. He had been accustomed to meet the men who became the revolutionaries on his way either to the Stephen's Green Club or the Arts Club in Upper Merrion Street in Dublin. 'That woman' was the Countess Constance Markiewicz (1861–1927). *Née* Gore-Booth, she was a daughter of one of the Sligo Big Houses, Lissadell (where Yeats stayed briefly in 1894), and married Count Casimir Duntin Markiewicz, a painter and Polish landowner from the Ukraine, whom she met when they were both art students in Paris. See also 'On a Political Prisoner', p. 228, and 'In Memory of Eva Gore-Booth and Con Markiewicz', p. 234. 'This man' was Patrick Pearse (1879–1916), a poet and barrister who founded St Enda's School, and was President of the provisional government in Dublin in 1916. His helper and friend was Thomas MacDonogh (1878–1916), a poet, dramatist and critic, who was a lecturer in University College, Dublin. John MacBride, described here as a drunken vainglorious lout, had fought against the British in the Boer war. Maud Gonne, who married him in 1903, sought a divorce from him in 1905 (for drunkenness and on other grounds) in the French courts, but, because he was officially resident in Ireland and she in France, she was given a separation. A stone of the heart shows the effect on Maud Gonne of long service to revolutionary politics.

There was some doubt in Ireland as to whether the English government would actually enact Home Rule, hence England 'may' keep faith. The Bill had received Royal Assent in 1914, but the Westminster government suspended its implementation until after the war was over. James Connolly (1870–1916), a trade union leader and organizer of the Irish Citizen Army, was military commander of the Republican forces in Dublin in 1916. The reference to green being worn is probably an echo of songs inspired by the 1798 revolution in Ireland, *The Wearing of the Green* and *Green on my Cape*.

p. 96 *On a Political Prisoner* refers to Constance Markiewicz (see notes on 'Easter 1916', p. 227). Her death sentence for taking part in the 1916 Rising was commuted and she was released from prison in 1917. When Yeats wrote this poem she was in Holloway gaol, London, for the second time, having been arrested for making seditious speeches as a Sinn Fein leader. On her release from prison she became the first woman to be elected an MP, though she did not take her seat at Westminster. She was Minister for Labour in the first and second Dail Eireann, but supported de Valera and the Republicans in the Civil War which occurred after the 1922 Treaty (which created the Irish Free State). Ben Bulben is a mountain to the north of Sligo. As a girl Constance Gore-Booth was known for her fearless horsemanship.

p. 97 *Towards Break of Day* is an account of dreams experienced by Yeats and his wife when they were staying at the Powerscourt Arms Hotel at Enniskerry, Co. Wicklow, in December 1918. The waterfall at Ben Bulben, north of Sligo, may be on the stream flowing into Glencar Lake. (Yeats and his wife had gone to see the waterfall in Powerscourt Demesne, which is not unlike the one in Sligo.) Mrs Yeats dreamed of the stag in 'The Tale of King Arthur' (in Sir Thomas Malory, *Works, III.* 5). Arthur was a mythical King of Britain, around whom the Arthurian legends are centred.

p. 98 *Demon and Beast* To 'pern' is to move with a circular spinning motion. Yeats noted that when he was a child in Sligo he could see a column of smoke from the 'pern mill' and was told 'pern' was another name for the spool on which thread was wound. To 'gyre' is to gyrate. In *A Vision* Yeats envisaged history as a series of opposing gyres of historical change. The portraits in the National Gallery, Dublin, are of Luke Wadding (1588–1657), an Irish Franciscan, President of the Irish College at Salamanca in Spain, who founded St Isodore's College in Rome; of the Ormondes, the titled members of the Butler family with which the Yeatses were proud to have a connection; and of Strafford, Sir Thomas Wentworth (1593–1641), the Lord Deputy of Ireland, 1632–40. The little lake is in St Stephen's Green, Dublin; the portly green-pated bird is a duck. The Thebaid and the Mareotic sea are in Egypt, regions where Christian monasticism flourished. Yeats read of St Anthony of Coma (c. 240–345), and of the monks in Flaubert's *La Tentatione de St Antoine* and in J. O. Hannay's *The Spirit and Origin of Christian Monasticism* and *The Wisdom of the Desert*. The Caesars are seen as threatened by Christianity, which Yeats regarded (see A p. 313) as their 'needed curb'.

p. 99 *The Second Coming* prophesies the coming of a new destructive god and the reversal of Christian values. The falconer symbolizes Christ (for gyre see notes on 'Demon and Beast' above). The Second Coming was predicted by Christ. (See Matthew xxiv, and see St John's description of the beast of the Apocalypse in Revelations.) *Spiritus Mundi* is a general storehouse of images no longer the property of a particular personality or spirit. Yeats associated his image of the rough beast (brazen and winged) with laughing, ecstatic destruction. Bethlehem, as Christ's birthplace, is a most holy place in Christian tradition.

p. 100 *A Prayer for my Daughter* was written a few weeks after the birth of Yeats's first child, Anne Butler Yeats, in February 1919. It is set by Yeats's tower in Galway, Gregory's Wood being part of Coole demesne. Helen of Troy found life in Sparta dull as the wife of Menelaus; she ran off with Paris, regarded here as a fool. (There is an implicit parallel with Maud Gonne, whom Yeats associated with Helen; her husband was described in 'Easter 1916' as a drunken lout.) The Queen is Aphrodite, who married Hephaestus. The Horn of Plenty refers to the cornucopia Zeus received from Amalthea, the goat who suckled him; her horns flowed with ambrosia and nectar. Yeats alludes to himself as having roved and loved and to the effect on him of his wife's 'glad kindness'. He attacks the effect of politics on Maud Gonne, the loveliest woman born.

THE TOWER

p 104 *Sailing to Byzantium* The first stanza describes Ireland. Yeats wrote about Byzantium (see *AV*(B), pp. 279–80) at about the end of the first Christian millennium: he imagined life after death existing there, and regarded the city as the centre of European civilization and the source of its spiritual philosophy. The 'sages' of the third stanza are related to the figures in the mosaic frieze in S. Apollinare in Ravenna. 'Perne in a gyre' is explained in the note on 'Demon and Beast', p. 228. The artificial bird of the fourth stanza has given rise to much comment (see *NC*, p. 215) and has many possible sources in Yeats's reading.

p. 105 *The Tower* Ben Bulben is a mountain north of Sligo. Yeats had begun to read Plato in translation in the 1890s; he also read Plotinus, being enthusiastic about Stephen MacKenna's five-volume translation (1917–30). Yeats noted that 'the persons mentioned are associated by legend, story or tradition with the neighbourhood of Thoor Ballylee or Ballylee Castle, where the poem was written. Mrs French lived at Peterswell in the eighteenth century and was related to Sir Jonah Barrington, who described the incident of the ears and the trouble that came of it', (*CP* 1950, p. 532). The peasant beauty and the blind poet are Mary Hynes and Antony Raftery, the blind Gaelic poet (1784–1834), and the incident of the man drowned in Cloone Bog, Co. Galway, is from Yeats's *Stories of Red Hanrahan*. 'The ghosts have been seen at their game of dice in what is now my bedroom, and the old bankrupt man lived about a hundred years ago. According to one legend he could only leave the Castle upon a Sunday because of his creditors, and according to another he hid in the secret passage.' (*CP* 1950, p. 532.) Edmund Burke (1729–97), the political philosopher, orator and politician, was Irish, as was Henry Grattan (1746–1820), a Protestant politician who had opposed the Act of Union (1800) and supported Catholic Emancipation (1829). Yeats said that in his passage on the Swan, in Part III, he had unconsciously echoed 'The Dying Swan' by his friend Thomas Sturge Moore (1870–1944).

p. 112 *Meditations in Time of Civil War* The second section describes Thoor Ballylee. See notes on 'The Phases of the Moon' p. 225 for *Il Penseroso*'s Platonist. The sword in the third section was given to Yeats by Junzo Sato, a Japanese who met him after a

lecture in Portland, Oregon (see also 'A Dialogue of Self and Soul').
The fifth section describes incidents in the Irish civil war, the
Irregulars being the members of the Irish Republican Army
opposed to the Anglo-Irish Treaty of 1922, the brown lieutenant
and his men members of the National Army loyal to the Pro-
visional Government. The 'stare' of the sixth section is a starling;
one built in a hole by Yeats's bedroom window during the Civil
War. Yeats's note on the seventh section reads 'a cry for vengeance
because of the murder of the Grand Master of the Templars seems
to me fit symbol for those who labour from hatred, and so for
sterility in various kinds . . . I suppose that I must have put hawks
into the fourth stanza because I have a ring with a hawk and a
butterfly upon it, to symbolize the straight road of logic, and so of
mechanism, and the crooked road of intuition: "For wisdom is a
butterfly and not a gloomy bird of prey".' (CP 1950, p. 534.)

p. 120 Nineteen Hundred and Nineteen This poem arose out of Lady
Gregory's account of some atrocities committed by Auxiliaries and
Black and Tans at Gort, Co. Galway, in the period before the
Treaty of 1922. The first section refers to the sacred olive at Athens
which grew miraculously fast after the Persians sacked and burnt
Athens in 480 BC. Phidias (c. 490–17 BC) was a famous Greek
sculptor. The golden grasshoppers and bees are described by the
Greek historian Thucydides (I, vi). The reference to an army being
a showy thing describes the peace before the First World War
(1914–18). The Acropolis was the citadel of Athens on which the
Erectheum and the Parthenon stood. In the second section Loie
Fuller (1862–1928) had a troupe of Japanese dancers and was known
for her dance with its whirling draperies manipulated by sticks. The
Platonic Year or Great Year is when the constellations return to the
positions from which they began. In the third section 'some mor-
alist' is probably Shelley, 'some Platonist' Thomas Taylor (1758–
1835), known as 'The Platonist', several of whose many transla-
tions Yeats read. The fourth section's 'seven years ago' probably
refers to the outbreak of the Great War in 1914; the poem was
written in 1921. The sixth section probably refers to the traditional
procession of witches on St John the Baptist's Eve. Robert Artisson
was the fourteenth-century incubus of Dame Alice Kyteler; Yeats
described him as 'an evil spirit much run after in Kilkenny at the

start of the fourteenth century'. Dame Alice Kyteler was condemned as a witch. In Holinshed's *Historie of Ireland* the sacrifice to the evil spirit was said to have been nine red cocks and nine peacocks' eyes.

p. 125 *The New Faces* was written to Lady Gregory; the new faces refer to her son Robert and his wife.

p. 125 *Two Songs from a Play* These two poems, sung by a chorus of musicians in Yeats's play *Resurrection*, illustrate Yeats's view that Christianity terminated a 2,000-year period of history and ushered in the beginnings of a new era with radical violence. The staring Virgin, Athene, snatched the heart from the body of Dionysus after he had been torn to pieces by the Titans, whom Zeus then killed. He swallowed the heart and begat Dionysus again upon the mortal Semele. The Muses sing because they regard the death and rebirth of the god as a recurring event. The second stanza refers to Virgil's fourth *Eclogue*, with its prophecy of the return of a golden age to earth. *Argo* was the ship in which Jason sailed on his quest for the golden fleece (the flashy bauble). The pagan Roman Empire is appalled because the world would become Christian and the Empire be destroyed. The virgin and her star refers to Mary, but links her with Athene and with Virgo, daughter of Jupiter and Themis, who carries the star Spica; Christ walks the room where the Last Supper took place. (See Matthew xxvi, 30; Mark xiv, 26; Luke xxii, 39 and John xviii, 1.) Babylonian starlight refers to the achievements of the city's astronomers and astrologists.

p. 127 *Leda and the Swan* deals with the union of god and mortal and the momentous births that ensue. (Zeus, father of the Greek gods, took the form of a swan and impregnated Leda, the wife of Tyndareus, King of Sparta; she bore twin sons, Castor and Pollux, and Helen.) The broken wall alludes to the sack of Troy by the Greeks. Agamemnon, King of Argos (leader with his brother Menelaus, King of Sparta, of the Greek force that went to Troy to bring Helen back to Sparta), was murdered on his return by his wife Clytemnestra (a daughter of Leda by Tyndareus) and her lover, Aegisthus.

p. 127 *Among School Children* records Yeats's reactions after visiting St Otteran's School in Waterford. He was then a Senator of the Irish Free State and wrote the poem on his 61st birthday. A Ledaean body refers to Maud Gonne. Plato's parable is in the *Symposium*. In writing 'Quattrocento finger' Yeats was thinking of Leonardo da Vinci's (1452–1519) work. Honey of generation is an image from *On the Cave of the Nymphs* by the Neoplatonic philosopher Porphy (*c.* 233–304). Aristotle (384–22 BC), the Greek philosopher, tutored Alexander the Great in Macedonia before returning to Athens, where he wrote most of his major works. Pythagoras, the sixth-century Greek philosopher, had, according to his biographer, Iamblichus, a golden thigh.

p. 130 *Colonus' Praise* is a translation of a chorus in *Oedipus at Colonus* by the Athenian dramatist Sophocles (*c.* 495–06 BC). Colonus of the horses was a deme or district in Athens, so called because the god Poseidon, who gave men the gift of horses, was worshipped there. Semele's lad was Dionysus (see note on 'Two Songs from a Play', p. 232). The gymnasts' garden was the Lycaeum, the site of the Academy founded by Plato. The olive tree in the Academy was reputed to have been the next to grow after the one on the Acropolis (see notes on 'Nineteen Hundred and Nineteen' p. 231). Athene was the patron goddess of Athens; she gave the olive to the city. The Great Mother was Demeter, who mourned for her daughter Persephone, carried into the underworld by Pluto (or Hades), where she spent half each year, returning to her mother for the other half. Cephisus is a river in Attica. Poseidon was god both of horses and of the sea.

p. 131 *Owen Aherne and his Dancers* This poem concerns Iseult Gonne, that young child; the first section was written four days, and the second seven days, after Yeats's marriage on 21 October 1917.

p. 133 *A Man Young and Old* 'First Love' refers to Maud Gonne, 'The Mermaid' to Diana Vernon. In 'From "Oedipus at Colonus"' the old wandering beggar is Oedipus and the God-hated children his daughters Antigone and Ismene.

p. 137 *All Souls' Night* The great Christ Church Bell is that of Christ Church in Oxford (where the Yeatses were living in 1920). All Souls' Night is usually 2 November, when members of the Roman Catholic Church pray for the souls of the faithful who are still in Purgatory. William Thomas Horton (1864–1919) produced mystical drawings for *The Yellow Book*; he had a Platonic relation-ship with Audrey Locke (1851–1916). Florence Farr Emery (d. 1917 in Ceylon) was a member of the group of students of the occult who gathered round MacGregor (originally Liddle) Mathers (1854–1918), author of *The Kabbalah Unveiled*. She acted in some of Yeats's plays and chanted his poems to the Psaltery. All three believed truth cannot be discovered but is revealed.

THE WINDING STAIR AND OTHER POEMS

P 141 *In Memory of Eva Gore-Booth and Con Markiewicz*. Lissadell was the Gore-Booth house in Sligo, where Yeats visited the two sisters in the winter of 1894–5.

p. 142 *Death* This poem was written on the assassination of Kevin O'Higgins (1892–1927), Minister of Justice in the Irish Free State.

p. 142 *A Dialogue of Self and Soul* is set in Yeats's tower. For Sato's blade see notes on 'Meditations in Time of Civil War' p. 230; the sword was made by Bishu Osafuné Motoshigé (Yeats refers to him, incorrectly, as Montashigi), who lived at Osafuné in the era of Oei (1394–1428).

p. 145 *Blood and the Moon* Some of the symbolism of this poem was suggested by the waste room at the top of Thoor Ballylee, where butterflies entered by the loopholes and died against the window-panes. The phrase half-dead at the top may have come from an anecdote about Swift, pointing at a tree the upper branches of which were withered, and saying that he would be like the tree, he would die at the top. Oliver Goldsmith (1728–74) was an Irish dramatist, poet, novelist and man of letters; the honeypot may be an allusion to *The Bee*, which he edited. The Dean is Jonathan Swift (1667–1745), Irish satirist, poet and letter-writer, whose writings exercised great political influence. In Yeats's play *The Words upon the Window-pane* he speaks in a seance. George Berkeley (1685–1753), Bishop of Cloyne, was an Immaterialist philosopher. For Burke see notes on 'The Tower' p. 230. *Saeva Indignatio* is a phrase from Swift's Epitaph (p. 152).

p. 147 *The Seven Sages* See notes on 'The Tower' p. 230 for Burke and Grattan, on 'Blood and the Moon', above, for Goldsmith and the Bishop of Cloyne (who believed in the efficacy of tar-water as a medicine). Stella was the name Swift gave Esther Johnson (d. 1728), whom he met at Sir William Temple's house, Moor Park; their friendship has caused much speculation (see Yeats's *The Words upon the Window-pane*, for instance). Swift's *Journal to Stella* consists of letters he wrote from London during 1710–13; he wrote a most moving account of her when she died and was buried in St Patrick's Cathedral, Dublin, of which he was Dean.

p. 149 *Coole Park, 1929* This poem celebrates the literary achievement of the Irish Renaissance and Lady Gregory's part in it. Coole Park was sold in 1927, and Lady Gregory lived in it until her death. The second stanza describes Douglas Hyde (1860–1949), founder of the Gaelic League, and first President of Eire, the author of *Love Songs of Connacht*; the 'manly pose' of Yeats himself; John Synge (1871–1909), the dramatist; and John Shawe-Taylor and Sir Hugh Lane, both nephews of Lady Gregory.

p. 150 *Coole Park and Ballylee, 1931* is another tribute to Lady Gregory, who died in 1932. 'Dark Raftery' is an allusion to the blindness of the Irish poet Antony Raftery (1784–1835).

p. 152 *Swift's Epitaph* is a translation of the Latin inscription in St Patrick's Cathedral, Dublin.

p. 152 *At Algeciras – A Meditation upon Death* Newton's metaphor is his comment on himself as being only like a boy playing on the seashore and diverting himself in now and then finding another or prettier shell than ordinary while the great ocean of truth lay undiscovered before him. Rosses' shore is in Sligo.

p. 153 *Byzantium* The prose draft is given in Yeats's *Pages from a Diary written in 1930*, p. 3, and his view of Byzantium in *AV*(B), p. 279. Hades' bobbin probably comes from Plato's *Republic*, which contains the myth of Er (cf. 'His Bargain', p. 162). The mummy-cloth, the birds, the flames, the dolphins are suggested in the prose craft: 'A walking mummy flames at the street corners where the soul is purified, birds of hammered gold singing in the golden trees, in the harbour [dolphins] offering their backs to the waiting dead that they may carry them to Paradise'.

p 155 *The Mother of God* Yeats had in his memory 'Byzantine mosaic pictures of the Annunciation, which show a line drawn from a star to the ear of the Virgin. She received the Word through the ear, a star fell, and a star was born.' (*CP* 1950, p. 536)

p. 155 *Vacillation* The tree in the second stanza derives from the *Mabinogion*. Attis was a vegetation god who castrated himself when Cybele the Earth Mother drove him to frenzy: his devotees castrated themselves at his March festival. The waters of Lethe (III), a river in Hades, enabled souls about to be reincarnated to forget their past lives. The great lord of Chou (VI) may be Chou-Kung, a twelfth-century member of the Chou dynasty. Isaiah's coal (VII) is described in Isaiah vi. Von Hügel (VIII) is the author of *The Mystical Elements of Religion* (2nd edition, 1927) which Yeats was reading at the time he wrote the poem; he is regarded as putting a Christian point of view.

WORDS FOR MUSIC PERHAPS

pp. 160–62 Crazy Jane was 'more or less founded' on cracked Mary, an old woman living in Gort, Co. Galway, a local satirist. 'Crazy Jane grown old looks at the Dancers' was suggested by a dream.

p. 163 In *Lullaby* the first stanza deals with Paris, the son of Priam, King of Troy. He was exposed as an infant by Priam as it was foretold he would bring ruin on Troy. He was brought up by shepherds and was asked to award the prize for beauty to one of three goddesses. Aphrodite promised him the fairest woman in the world if she won the prize, and he subsequently persuaded Helen, wife of Menelaus, King of Sparta, to elope with him. Tristram in the second stanza is the son of the King of Lyonesse, who falls in love with Iseult, daughter of the King of Ireland. He leaves Ireland, but is sent back there by King Mark, to ask Iseult to marry King Mark. She marries him, but a love potion makes her love and Tristram's irresistible. Tristram leaves eventually but is killed by Mark as he is harping to Iseult. The Eurotas is a river in Sparta where Zeus in the form of a swan mated with Leda (see notes on 'Leda and the Swan' p. 232).

p. 164 *Mad as the Mist and Snow* Yeats lists Horace (65–8 BC), the Roman poet, Homer (?between 1050 and 850 BC), the Greek epic poet, Plato (*c*.427–*c*.348 BC) the Greek philosopher, and Tully or

Marcus Tulius Cicero (106–43 BC) the Roman orator, politician and letter-writer.

p. 165 *I am of Ireland* is founded on a fourteenth-century lyric 'Icham of Irlaunde'.

p. 166 *The Delphic Oracle on Plotinus* is based on the verse oracle in Porphyry's *Life of Plotinus*, describing Plotinus' whereabouts; in the poem he is making the symbolic return journey through the sea of life, and being welcomed by the Judges of the Underworld and 'the spirits pleasing to the Gods – Plato, Pythagoras and all the people of the Choir of Immortal Love'. The poem is very close to Stephen MacKenna's translation of Plotinus (205–70), who was born in Egypt, died at Alexandria and opened a school at Rome; he was the founder of Neoplatonic philosophy. Rhadamanthus was a son of Zeus and Europa, renowned for his impartial justice. Porphyry describes Minos, Rhadamanthus and Deacus, the sons of God, as enthroned as judges of souls. Minos was also a son of Zeus by Europa.

A WOMAN YOUNG AND OLD

p. 167 *Father and Child* is about Anne Yeats, the man being Fergus Fitzgerald. The children were seven or eight at the time Yeats wrote the poem, which echoes George Herbert's 'The Collar': 'I struck the board, and cry'd, No more.'

p. 168 *Her Triumph* may be related to the Bordone picture *St George and the Dragon* (see notes on 'Michael Robartes and the Dancer' p. 226) and to Perino del Vaga's *Roma* in the Papal apartments at Castel S. Angelo. Perseus killed Medusa the gorgon, and rescued Andromeda from a dragon.

p. 169 *Chosen* may refer to Plato's myth of Er, in which the souls of men and women choose the lots which govern their future destinies. Yeats remarked in 1929 that he had symbolized a woman's life as the struggle of the darkness to keep the sun from rising from its earthly bed: he changed the symbol in the second stanza to that of the souls of men and women ascending through the Zodiac. He had read that the whorl 'changes into a sphere at one of the points where the Milky Way crosses the Zodiac'.

p. 170 *Her Vision in the Wood* The wounded man on the litter may

238 SELECTED POETRY

be Adonis. The beast may be the boar that killed Adonis, a beautiful youth loved by Aphrodite. Andrea Mantegna (1431–1506) lived mainly at Mantua; he painted *The Agony in the Garden*.

p. 173 From the 'Antigone' is a translation based upon the work of several other translators, particularly upon the French version by Paul Masqueray. Parnassus, a mountain a few miles from Delphi, was sacred to the Muses (one peak was sacred to Apollo, the other to Dionysus). The Empyrean was the highest part of the supposedly spherical heavens. Antigone was the child of Oedipus; she committed suicide in the *Antigone* of Sophocles.

A FULL MOON IN MARCH

p. 174 *Parnell's Funeral* This poem refers to the star which fell at Parnell's funeral in 1891 at Glasnevin Cemetery, Dublin. The 'Great Comedian' is the Irish politician Daniel O'Connell (1775–1847). The poem also refers to a vision described in Yeats's *Autobiographies*, p. 372. For Emmet, Fitzgerald and Tone see notes on 'September 1913', p. 221. Eamon de Valera, President of Eire (1959–75), took part in the 1916 Rising, was President of the Sinn Fein Party (1917–26), and then President of the Fianna Fail Party (1926–59). William T. Cosgrave (1889–1966) was President of Dail Eireann (1922–32). Eoin O'Duffy (1892–1944) was Director of the Blue Shirt organization.

p. 176–9 *Supernatural Songs* In 'Ribh at the Tomb of Baile and Aillinn', Ribh was 'an imaginary critic of St Patrick'. The group of 'Supernatural Songs' is commented on by Yeats in *The King of the Great Clock Tower* (1934), p. 44. Baile and Aillinn were each given false news of the other's death by Aengus, the Celtic god of Love; they died of broken hearts, and turned into swans linked by a golden chain; a yew tree and an apple tree grew over their respective graves. In 'Meru' the twin of Mount Meru is Mount Kailasa in Tibet; it is the centre of paradise in Hindu mythology. Everest is in the Himalayas on the borders of Tibet and Nepal.

LAST POEMS

p. 180 *The Gyres* 'Old Rocky Face' was probably Shelley's Ahasuerus in *Hellas*. For gyres see note on 'Demon and Beast' p. 228. Empedocles (c. 490–30 BC) was a Greek philosopher who

regarded all things as composed of earth, air, fire and water, min-
gled by love or separated by strife. For Hector see note on 'The
Phases of the Moon'. p. 225.

p. 181 *Lapis Lazuli* This piece of lapis lazuli belonged to Yeats.
King Billy is William of Orange, and the reference to bomb-balls is
to a ballad 'The Battle of the Boyne'. The Shakespearean characters
do not weep like the hysterical women of the first line. Yeats cited
Lady Gregory's belief that tragedy must be a joy to the man who
dies. Callimachus was a late fifth-century BC sculptor, inventor of
the running drill, who made a golden lamp for the Erectheum.

p. 183 *An Acre of Grass* A description of Riversdale, Rathfarnham,
Co. Dublin, Yeats's home from 1932 to his death.

p. 184 *Beautiful Lofty Things* For John O'Leary see notes on 'Sep-
tember 1913' p. 221. Yeats's father, the artist John Butler Yeats
(1839–1922), spoke in the debate at the Abbey Theatre in 1907, on
the issues arising from the riots about Synge's *The Playboy of the
Western World*. Standish O'Grady (1846–1925) was an influential
Irish historian and novelist. Lady Gregory's reaction to a threat of
death from one of her tenants is described. Howth is north of
Dublin on the north side of the peninsula which forms the northern
arm of Dublin Bay. Yeats may have been remembering the day he
spent there with Maud Gonne in 1891, after she rejected his first
proposal of marriage.

p. 185 *The Curse of Cromwell* Yeats regarded Oliver Cromwell
(1599–1658) as the Lenin of his day. His exploits in Ireland are
notorious: he sacked Drogheda and Wexford; by a Settlement Act
(1652) and a Sequestration Act (1653) only Clare and Connaught
were left in the possession of Irish landowners, and about eleven
million acres out of the twenty million remaining were confiscated.
The phrase 'beaten into the clay' comes from Frank O'Connor's
translation *Kilcash*. The Spartan boy stole a fox and let it gnaw him
to death under his clothes rather than have his crime detected; the
story is told by the Greek historian Plutarch (*c*. 46–120) in his *Lives
of Ten Orators*.

p. 186 *Come Gather Round Me, Parnellites* Parnellites supported
Parnell after his divorce case (see notes on 'To a Shade', p. 222). A
lass was Mrs O'Shea, whom Parnell married. See Yeats's views in
E & I, pp. 486–90.

p. 190 *The Pilgrim* refers to a legendary evil spirit, 'a long-legged bird with no feathers on its wings', seen at Lough Derg by pilgrims on the pilgrimage to St Patrick's cave (where he is supposed to have fasted and had a vision of the next world).

p. 191 *The Municipal Gallery Revisited* The paintings in this poem are identified in Arland Ussher, *Yeats and the Municipal Gallery*, 1959, and in Jeffares, *NC*, pp. 398–402.

p. 194 *Are You Content?* The second stanza refers in turn to Yeats's great-grandfather (*ll.* 9, 10), his grandfather (*ll.* 11–12), his grand-father's brother-in-law and family, the Corbets, who lived in Sandymount Castle, Dublin (*l.* 13), his maternal grandfather (*ll.* 13, 14), and that grandfather's father-in-law (*l.* 15). The Butler connec-tion (*l.* 15) was formed when Benjamin Yeats married Mary Butler in 1773.

p. 195 *The Statues* Yeats is saying that the Pythagorean doctrine of numbers paved the way for the art of Greek sculptors, who carved statues by exact measurements. He argues that Europe was not born when the Greek galleys defeated the Persian hordes at Salamis (480 BC) but when 'the Doric studios sent out those broad-backed marble statues against the multiform, vague, expressive Asiatic sea, they gave to the sexual instinct of Europe its goal, its fixed type' (*E & I*, p. 451). The one image refers to the effect of the Greek sculptors who followed Alexander the Great to India (both on modern sculptors, Yeats commented, and on the great seated Bud-dha). The idea of a thin Hamlet came from Yeats's seeing the part played by thin actors (Sir Henry Irving among others). Crimalkin is a name for a cat (a combination of grey and malkin, an archaic word for a cat). For Pearse see notes on 'Easter 1916', p. 227. Pearse was in the General Post Office in the 1916 Rising. Yeats thought his own revival of Gaelic mythology had inspired a cult of Cuchulain, the Irish hero of the Red Branch tales. Yeats sees Pearse as bringing past forces and skills into being again, so that the Irish will return to heroic proportions, and thus gain artistic and intellectual independence.

p. 196 *News for the Delphic Oracle* This poem describes Poussin's *The Marriage of Peleus and Thetis*, in the National Gallery of Ireland (it is now entitled *Acis and Galatea*), adding Oisin and Niamh to its ironic pictures of after-life, according to Neoplatonic doctrine. Niamh, the fairy princess who spirited Oisin, son of Finn, away to three enchanted islands for three hundred years in Yeats's *The Wanderings of Oisin* (1889) is described as a man-picker because she arrived on a horse and told Finn she had come 'That I might have your son to kiss'. Pythagoras was a sixth-century BC Greek philosopher who argued for the transmigration of souls and investigated the relations of numbers. Plotinus (205–70), born in Egypt, opened a school at Rome and was the founder of Neoplatonic philosophy. 'Those Innocents' may be the Holy Innocents, the male children under two whom Herod had killed in an attempt to eliminate Jesus Christ. Peleus captured and married Thetis, a Nereid; their marriage was celebrated on Mount Pelion and their surviving son was the hero Achilles.

p. 197 *Long-Legged Fly* Caius Julius Caesar, the Roman general, statesman and historian, lived from 102 to 44 BC; the title Caesar was given to Roman emperors from Augustus to Hadrian. The topless towers are those of Troy. Maud Gonne is described as 'part woman, three parts a child'. The third stanza refers to Michaelangelo's painting the ceiling in the Sistine Chapel in Rome (see notes on 'Michael Robartes and the Dancer', p. 226).

p. 198 *A Bronze Head* The poem refers to a statue of Maud Gonne by Laurence Campbell, RHA, in the Municipal Gallery of Modern Art, Dublin. The philosopher J. McT. E. McTaggart (1866–1925) is described as profound; Yeats read several of his books.

p. 200 *Why should not Old Men be Mad?* The girl is Iseult Gonne; Helen is Maud Gonne.

p. 201 *The Circus Animals' Desertion* refers to Yeats's *The Wanderings of Oisin* (1889), a narrative poem drawing on Gaelic legends, and to Yeats's plays *The Countess Kathleen* (1892), written for Maud Gonne, and *On Baile's Strand* (1930), which deals with Cuchulain's death.

p. 203 *Politics* This poem was prompted by Archibald MacLeish's praise of Yeats's language as public. Yeats here answers MacLeish's comment that Yeats was unable to use this public language on politics.

p. 203 *The Man and the Echo* The cleft called Alt is on Knocknarea, a mountain in Sligo. The play is *Cathleen ni Houlihan* (1902), which had an electrifying effect on its audience. The woman is Margot Collis (the episode of her madness is described in Jeffares *YANB*, p. 331) and the house is Coole Park.

p. 205 *Under Ben Bulben* The 'sages' are the hermits of the Thebaid, referred to in 'Demon and Beast'; Shelley's Witch of Atlas sees 'the reality of things', according to Yeats's essay on Shelley's poetry, as she passes 'by Moeris and the Mareotic Lakes'. The horsemen may be the visionary beings whom Mary Battle, a Sligo servant, used to describe to Yeats. John Mitchel (1815–75) was parodying the daily Order of Service, 'Give us peace in our time, O Lord', in his *Jail Journal* (1854). The comment on measurement relates to *The Statues* (p. 195) and that on Michaelangelo to *Long-Legged Fly* (p. 197). Edward Calvert (1799–1883) was an English visionary artist, Richard Wilson (1714–82) a landscape painter and Claude Lorrain (1600–82) a French landscape artist, expert in the picturesque. Yeats died near Roquebrune in France in January 1939 and was buried in the cemetery there, to be subsequently reinterred in Sligo in 1948. His great-grandfather John Yeats had been a rector of Drumcliff.

SELECT BIBLIOGRAPHY

BIOGRAPHICAL STUDIES

Richard Ellmann, *The Man and the Masks* (1948; 2nd edn. 1979)

Joseph Hone, *W. B. Yeats, 1865–1939* (1942; rev. edn. 1962)

A. Norman Jeffares, *W. B. Yeats: man and poet* (1949; rev. edn. 1962)

A Norman Jeffares, *W. B. Yeats. A New Biography* (1988; rev. edn. 1990)

John Kelly, '"Friendship is all the house I have": Lady Gregory and W. B. Yeats' in *Lady Gregory, Fifty Years After,* ed. Ann Saddlemyer and Colin Smythe (1987)

Augustine Martin, *W. B. Yeats* (1983; rev. edn. 1990)

William M. Murphy, *Prodigal Father: the Life of John Butler Yeats, 1839–1922* (1978)

Frank Tuohy, *Yeats* (1976)

SOME BASIC YEATS TEXTS

Autobiographies (1955); *Collected Poems* (1933; 1950); *Yeats's Poems*, ed. A Norman Jeffares (1989); *Collected Plays*, (1934; 1952); *Essays and Introductions* (1961); *Explorations* (1962); *Memoirs*, ed. Denis Donoghue (1972); *Mythologies* (1959); *The Senate Speeches of W. B. Yeats*, ed. Donald R. Pearce (1960); *Uncollected Prose by W. B. Yeats* I, ed. John P. Frayne (1970), II, ed. John P. Frayne and Colton Johnson (1975); *A Vision* (1925; 1937; and 1978, ed. George Mills Harper and Walter Kelly Hood).

CORRESPONDENCE

The Letters of Yeats, ed. Allan Wade (1954); *The Collected Letters of W. B. Yeats*, I *1865–1895*, ed. John Kelly and Eric Domville (1986)

Letters on Poetry from W. B. Yeats to Dorothy Wellesley (1940)

J. B. Yeats, *Letters to His Son W. B. Yeats and Others, 1869–1922*, ed. Joseph Hone (1944)

SOME CRITICAL STUDIES

Dennis Donoghue, *Yeats* (1971)

Richard Ellmann, *The Identity of Yeats* (1954)

T. R. Henn, *The Lonely Tower* (1950; rev. edn. 1965)

Graham Hough, *The Mystery Religion of W. B. Yeats* (1984)

A. Norman Jeffares, *A New Commentary on the Poems of W. B. Yeats* (1984)

A Norman Jeffares, *The Circus Animals* (1970)

B. Rajan, *Yeats: A Critical Introduction* (1965)

Jon Stallworthy, *Between the Lines: Yeats's Poetry in the Making* (1963)

A. G. Stock, *W. B. Yeats: His Poetry and Thought* (1961; rev. edn. 1964)

Peter Ure, *Yeats* (1963)

INDEX TO TITLES

INDEX TO FIRST LINES

251